Columbia University Contributions
to Anthropology
Volume XXIV

CATAWBA TEXTS
By
FRANK G. SPECK

CATAWBA TEXTS

BY

FRANK G. SPECK

AMS PRESS
NEW YORK

Reprinted with the permission of
Columbia University Press
From the edition of 1934, New York
First AMS EDITION published 1969
Manufactured in the United States of America

Library of Congress Catalogue Card Number: 77-82345

AMS PRESS, INC.
New York, N. Y. 10003

CONTENTS

Introduction . . . . **X**
Explanation of symbols for sounds used in the texts . . . . **XVI**

I. MYTHS AND TALES 1
  1. U'gni, the Comet 1
    (a) The Bad Woman Who Stole a Boy and Became a
       Comet (III) 1
    (b) The Eagle Kidnapper, the Pileated Woodpecker,
       U'gni, the Comet and the Sky Rope (II) 3
    (c) The Eagle Kidnapper. Variant (II) 4
  2. Origin of the Red Winged Blackbird and Dove (III) . . . 4
  3. How Pileated Woodpecker Got his Red Crest and
    Robin his Red Breast (II) 5
  4. How Yellow Hammer Got her White Inner Wings (II) 5
  5. How the Wolf was Frightened and Became Wild (II) 6
  6. How Opossum Lost his Bushy Tail (II) 7
  7. How Tree Frog Taught Toad to Cry (II). 7
  8. How Chipmunk Got his Stripes (II) 8

Rabbit Tales
  9. (a) Rabbit Steals the Fire from the Buzzards (II) . . 8
    (b) Variant (III) 9
 10. Rabbit Steals Water from the Snapping Turtle (II) 10
 11. Rabbit and Snail Go for a Doctor (I) 11

Terrapin Tales
 12. How Terrapin Married Chief's Daughter and Made
    an Ice House. (II) 11
 13. Race between Deer and Terrapin (I) 13
 14. Recitative from Story of Bull Frog, Terrapin and
    Snail go to Bring Doctor Toad (IV) 13
 15. Logger-head Terrapin, the Snake and the Man (III) 14

Miscellaneous Tales
 16. Opossum Tricks the Deer and the Wolves (III) 15
 17. The Deer and the Sleeping Hunter (III) 17
 18. Deer Jumps across Catawba River (II) 18
 19. Fox and Raccoon (III). 18
 20. Hawk and Buzzard (III) 19

21. Buzzard Steals Fish (II) 19
22. The Bear and Wolf on the Mountain (II).......... 20
23. Tree Frog and Bull Frog Compete in Crying (III)... 20
24. The Boy who was Raised with the Hogs (II) 21
25. A Boy Eats a Partridge Raw (III) 22
26. The Child-Eating Alligator (II) 22
27. The Flood (II) 23

Witchcraft

28. A Cherokee Witch in the Form of an Owl (II) 24
29. A Cherokee Wrestles with his Wife who is a Witch (II) 24
30. The Woman who Became an Owl (II)............. 25
31. The Women who Escaped by Transforming Themselves into Animals (II) 26
32. The Mischievous Dwarfs and How to Avert Them (II) 26

Historic Narrations

33. Revenge on the Shawnee Raiders (II) 28
34. A Dog Tells how the Tuscarora Killed his People (II) 28
35. The Catawba Kill a Chickasaw and Put him inside his Horse's Belly (III) 29
36. The Woman, the Deer, and the Wolf (II) 30

II. FOLK BELIEFS 30

Reptiles

37. Legend of the Ancient Indian Town and the Monster Water Serpent (II)............................. 32
38. Monster Water Snake Crushes Children (III)........ 33
39. The Monster Leech (III) 33
40. The Glass Snake (III) 33
41. The Whip Snake (III) 34
42. The Salamander Barking — a Death Omen (III) ... 34

Birds

43. The Wren Causes Laziness (III)................... 34
44. The Wren is Lazy (III) 35
45. Bird Calls a Sign of Someone Coming (I) 35
46. The Whippoorwill's Hat is the Lady Slipper (III) ... 35
47. The Humming Bird was Made from Man's Breath (III) 35
48. Seeing the Cardinal Denotes an Unexpected Occurrence (III) 36
49. The Errant Blue Jay (III) 36
50. Owls Crying are Omens of Good News (III)........ 36

Charms

51. Nature Rejoicing after a Storm (III) 37
52. A Prayer Charm for Good Weather (II) 38
53. The Rabbit's Foot as a Love Charm (I) 38
54. Red Blossom for Luck Charm (III) 38

Omens

55. The Ground Hog and His Shadow (III) 38
56. The Omen of the Falling Star (II)............... 39
57. Snow Birds a Sign of Snow or Sleet (III) 39
58. Crows Cawing Means Clear Weather (III) 39
59. When Red Root Blossoms Terrapin Lays its Eggs(III) 40
60. Sign of Burning Soot in the Chimney 40
61. Dreams of Luck 40
62. How to Avert Bad Luck when Meeting a Woman
    While Hunting (III) 41

Miscellaneous Beliefs

63. Sticks Turn into Snakes to Guard a Melon Patch (III) 41
64. Thrust Iron into Fire to Drive away Witch Owl (III) 41
65. Belief Concerning Crawfish in Springs (II) 42
66. How Storms Arise in the Mountains (III) 42
67. Ghosts (III) 42

Prayers

68. Prayer to Avert a Thunder Storm (II)............ 43
69. Prayer to Avert a Cyclonic Storm (III) 43
70. Prayer for Night's Rest (III) 44
71. Supplication (III) 44

Taboos

72. Against Going into a Corn Crib for Three Days after
    a Death (I) 44
73. Against Burning Sassafras Wood (I) 45
74. Against Making Fire and Smoke before the Moon (III) 45
75. Taboo for Widows (I) 45
76. Against Cooking Deer and Turkey Meat Together (II) 45

Songs

77. (a) Song Used when Washing Children in the
    Creek (II).................................... 46
    (b) Verse for Blind Man's March Game (II) 46

III. MEDICINE PRACTICES 47
  78. Ghosts the Cause of Disease (III) 47
  79. Sickness Caused from Eating Clay (III) 47
  80. Medicine Blowing by a Catawba Doctor (III) 48
  81. Singing when Giving Medicine (III) 49
  82. Sucking as a Remedial Measure (III) 50
  83. Enema to Relieve Constipation (III) 50
  84. Scratching the Shoulder with Garfish Teeth for
     Strength (III) 51
  85. Rules for Gathering Herbs (III) 51
  86. Gathering Medicines and Praying (III) 52
  87. Gathering Medicines in the Full of the Moon (III).... 52
  88. Herbal Remedies (III) 53

IV. SOCIAL CUSTOMS 64

Dances
  89. The Catawba Round Dance (I) 64
  90. The Catawba Horse Dance (I) 64
  91. The Wild Goose Dance (III) 65
  92. The Bear Dance (III) 66

Marriage
  93. On Marriage of Close Kin (III) 66

Death
  94. Burial Beneath the House, Giving the Ghost a Drink
     of Water, and the Watch for Three Days after
     Death (III) 67

Personal Narratives.
  95. Mrs. Owl's Recollection of Going to Church (I) 68
  96. Famine Time (III) 68
  97. Catawba Poverty (III) 69

V. INDUSTRIES AND OCCUPATIONS 70
  98. How the Catawba Make Pots and Pipes (I) 70
  99. How Cane Baskets are Made (I) 72
  100. Tanning Process (III) 72
  101. Catching Fish by Use of Poison (I) 73
  102. Fish Shooting with Bow and Arrow (I) 74
  103. Trapping Fish with Baskets (I) 75
  104. Formula to Make Fish Bite. (II) 76
  105. Bird Brushing (III) 76

106. Bush Netting (III) 78
107. Opossum Hunting (III) 79
108. Making Corn-Husk Mats (III).................... 79

Preparation of Food
109. Recipe for Parched Corn Soup (III) 80
110. Recipe for Lye Hominy (III) 80
111. Rules for Cooking Beans (I)..................... 81
112. Rules for Cooking Crawfish (I) 81
113. Rules for Cooking Hoe Cakes (I) 81

Supplement
114. Rabbit Fails to Imitate his Host, the Bear 83
115. Opossum Outwits the Deer and the Wolf 84
116. The Pig Outwits the Wolf 88
117. How the Ghosts were Heard Dancing 91

INTRODUCTION

The Indians of the once famous Catawba Nation, inhabiting the upper waters of the river bearing their name in North and South Carolina have been a center of interest for American linguists and ethnologists for almost a century. It was Albert Gallatin who in 1836 first called attention to the peculiarities of Catawba and its difference from neighboring languages, and who in the first attempt to list American Indian tongues gave it an independent position. In 1881 Dr. Albert S. Gatschet of the Bureau of American Ethnology discovered its relation with the Siouan languages which was accepted by Mr. J. O. Dorsey (See Powell, 7th Annual Report Bureau of Ethnology, 1891), and rediscovered by Dr. A. F. Chamberlain (1886)[1]. Gatschet then devoted himself to the preparation of a grammatical sketch of Catawba and a word list which was extended by Dr. J. R. Swanton of the Bureau of American Ethnology. His grammatical sketch appeared in the American Anthropologist, N. S. Vol. 2, No. 3, 1900.

Nothing of particular note was then done upon the task of analyzing Catawba until after 1910, when, by the turn of fate, the language had neared the precipice of oblivion which it has now practically reached. By this time Billy George, the last of the Catawba men of the old régime who had helped Gatschet with his study in 1881 had died, and the remaining members of the tribe who were still conversant with the language were not rhetorically fluent in their native idiom. My own first contact with a Catawba informant was in 1913 with Mrs. Samson Owl, who left the Catawba reservation upon her marriage with a Cherokee and moved to the home of the latter in the mountains of western North Carolina. A short collection of texts was taken by me from Mrs. Owl's dictation without prior knowledge on my part of the grammatical structure of the language. This material was published in 1913[2]. Dr. Swanton subsequently visited the Catawba reservation in the interests of the Bureau of American Ethnology and recorded grammatical and lexical material

---

[1] Chamberlain, A. F., The Affinities of the Catawba Language. Toronto, 1888. He independently pronounced Catawba to be a branch of the Siouan stock of languages.

[2] Speck, F. G. Some Catawba Texts and Folk Lore. JAFL. Vol. XXVI, No. CII, 1913.

from several speakers of the language then living there[1]. A trip was also made by Dr. Michelson to interrogate sources on the reservation. No other work was attempted with Mrs. Owl until my return to her home in 1921 through funds supplied by the Bureau. These were renewed in 1922 and 1923. Provision was also made at the same time by the Bureau to include text recording from Margaret Brown, who was then living on the Catawba reservation, and her daughter Sally (Mrs. Gordon). In 1928 the Council of Learned Societies made an appropriation to continue this important task to 1931, as occasion arose for me to undertake it during spare time available from University duties. The results of these periods of work are now made available in collected form to remain as a foundation for grammatical analysis of a now defunct Siouan language. The texts are marked with the individuality in style and fluency of their narrators. I shall mention some of these varied qualities later. To identify them, the narratives in the collection are numbered by Roman numeral references indicated in parentheses following the titles:

I. Mrs. Samson Owl (née Susan Harris) living at Cherokee, North Carolina, aged 83 in 1930, narrator of 21 tales. She was born at the mouth of Sugar (Sugeree) Creek on Catawba River above the Catawba reservation, York County, South Carolina.

II. Mrs. Margaret Wiley Brown of the Catawba Nation who spent her life on the reservation, and died in 1922 at the age of 85, narrator of 33 texts.

Mrs. Brown said that among the older people she was known when a young girl by the Indian sobriquet of *E'ntini· hi·nowa"*, "Anthony's daughter". Her father was a very old man when he died, as she thought, in about 1845. He bore the marks of smallpox, evidence of his being a victim of the epidemic of 1800. Mrs Brown through him had her bringing-up under circumstances which should have left her a far deeper memory heritage of native institutions had she been a woman of better mentality.

III. Mrs. Sally Gordon, (née Sally Brown), daughter of Margaret Brown (II) of the Catawba reservation, born 1865, narrator of 62 texts.

IV. Sam Brown, son of Margaret Brown (II) who, although not responsible for complete text dictations, rendered invaluable service by interpreting and acting as personnel manager of his women folk, born 1873.

---

[1] Swanton, J. R. Catawba Notes, Journal of the Washington Academy of Sciences, Vol. VIII, No. 19, 1918.

It is apparent from findings for which Dr. Swanton should be credited, that Catawba with Woccon and the dialects of Chicora and Duhare, falls into a southern subdivision of languages and dialects within the larger southeastern Siouan grouping, as the latter was proposed and defined by James Mooney of the Bureau of American Ethnology in 1894. This leaves Tutelo and Saponi, with other Siouan tongues spoken in that part of the southeastern area from North Carolina through the Virginia plateau region, to form a northern subdivision of the southeastern Siouan idioms. These conclusions are outlined with contributory evidence in several separate articles by Dr. Swanton[1] and myself[2].

While the literary merit of the Catawba tales and narratives may indeed be low, the same cannot be said of the historical or philological value of the dictations. No more specimens of Catawba speech may henceforth be hoped for from native sources. Regrettable as the circumstances are, the fact remains that scarcely a score of Catawba terms, and these at best badly pronounced, could be recorded from the one hundred remaining members of the tribe now living on and around the reservation. The language is gone..

Texts dictated by Indian narrators are inevitably much like other classes of spontaneous literary product in their arrangement of thought, the choice of subject, the scope of ideas and in their fullness or meagerness of expression. Much depends upon the personality of the narrator. And some of them dictate with deliberation and clearness. In groups where it is possible to choose individuals to serve as dictating informants some consideration can be given to their qualities of intellect and power of expression. This was not possible in the case of the Catawba, since there have been but four persons living during the period of my investigation who were capable of expressing themselves in their native tongue. Three of them were women, one a man, which circumstance might ordinarily be expected to have been of advantage in recording the last echoes of a dying speech, inasmuch as women are better talkers and better versed in the knowledge which the ethnologist desires to preserve. But of the three, two, Margaret Wiley Brown and her daughter, Sally Brown Gordon, happened to be women of unusually low intelligence. In recording information of this character from native dictation one often finds himself dealing with individuals endowed with qualities really intellectual, so far as unsophisticated groups

[1] Swanton, J. R. New Light on the Early History of the Siouan Peoples, Journal of the Washington Academy of Sciences, Vol. 13, No. 3, 1923.

[2] Speck, F. G. The Possible Siouan Identity of the Words Recorded from Francisco of Chicora on the South Carolina Coast. Journal of the Washington Academy of Sciences, Vol. 14, No. 13, 1924.

can nurture such qualities, and still more often with those who are extremely intelligent. But truth compels me to confess that Margaret Brown fell into neither of these catagories. This condition had its effect upon the text narratives recorded from her.

Mrs. Susan Harris Owl, although an exception to the foregoing classification, was handicapped from the ethnological angle of estimate by extreme religious prejudices. And as for Sam Brown, my only male narrator, who realized his inability to dictate fluently, he had the good sense to act in the capacity of mediator. Without his aid his mother and sister would have been incoherent. I may even go so far as to ascribe the success of text recording during the last three years largely to his help, so admirably did he manage the task of focusing the attention of his sister upon our work. Circumstances like those outlined seldom confront the linguist studying in the field. And it is better that they be mentioned in the introduction in order that due allowance be made in estimating the character of Catawba thought and its expression as well, as they come to light in the texts that follow. Personally, it is my own feeling that the characteristics of staccato style and poorly united expression, so apparent in the narratives, are typical of Catawba thought complexes covering a period of at least fifty years. I reach this conclusion after an examination of the linguistic material recorded by Dr. Gatchet in the 80's, from the standard of which my material seems not to have deviated to any considerable extent. And in addition it may be noted that his major informant was Billy George, then an extremely old man whose memory went back into the early part of the 19th century to a period when the morale of the tribe and presumably the spirit of the language could not have been affected detrimentally by contact with English-speaking Europeans. In support of this supposition it should also be added that my three women informants had spoken the language continuously and, it is claimed, fluently in their younger days when there were still a number of older people whose constant habit was to speak Catawba. Nevertheless a strong impression is gained by close analysis of the style and the composition of the texts offered here that their experience with the language, if not their memory of it, had been seriously affected for the worse. To the student of Siouan languages there is nothing strange in the lack of clarity, in the ambiguity of reference in direct and indirect discourse, in the references to person characterizing its verbal morphology. Yet to me these weaknesses, defects perhaps, are more than usually conspicuous in Catawba. It may be archaism; it may be due to collapse. Biloxi impresses me as being open to approach from a similar angle.

With the introduction of schooling upon the Catawba reservation, hardly more than a generation ago, has come a momentous change in the conditions of culture. The younger Indians are a different people from those of even their parents' generation. They possess practically no knowledge of the native tales and traditions which made animal life and nature in general so mysterious to their ancestors. Indeed they had no interest in the treasures of a literary heritage until my coming among them. Only in the minds of about a dozen of those ther over fifty years of age, who were still illiterate, was there a residuum of native belief to differentiate their attitude toward the world from that of the modern prosaic school-children who know that the sun does not move majestically across the sky, that the comet can not by any flash of the imagination be that great hero of mythology, Ugni, falling from the rope that he stretched to the realm above to carry him and his mother there, that the whippoorwill does not refrain from uttering his spring call until the lady's slipper has blossomed so that he can use it for his hat, that the saying regarding the little wild dwarfs inhabiting the old Catawba village ruins are mere superstitions. For the older people referred to the only source of education was the lore of their forbears, a picturesque and highly imaginative body of learning with the characteristics of classical creative explanation which has yielded place to the universal facts of the primary school text book. In consequence the young, though literate, have lost the charm of personality, and even the outlook on the world that marks the mentality of their elders. Unfortunate anomalies! It is, however, no place to carry such comparisons further. There would be no occasion to speak of them were it not for the need of a few comments upon the estimable simple and affectionate elderly persons who unconsciously through ignorance of school teachings have preserved for us the fragments of age-old Catawba nature-reasoning that appear in these pages. To them the animal heroes are still the „ancient terrible ones (*dəpə-*)", as the syllables imply (the same in Biloxi). Ugni and the sky-rope has Siouan analogies; but aside from this there are few tales to connect Catawba types with those beyond the southeastern frontier.

The Catawba texts, a last feeble voice from the grave of a defunct native culture of the southeast, are presented with a certain after-sense of satisfaction, not caused by the manner in which they are handled but in having had the opportunity to preserve them for future students of human achievement in its simpler phases.

The ethnological material embodied in the texts, together with what was directly recorded and observed during my period of residence with the tribe as work went on, is reserved for separate handling in a subsequent memoir.

The widespread custom in North America of restraint against reciting tales in summer times lest snakes overhear and punish the tellers by lying in wait and biting them is varied in Catawba in the following manner.

We learn here that to narrate after dark is to invite annoyance from snakes. Should a snake hear a person relating tales it will lie in wait in the path to bite him or her. The same danger applies to telling stories in the summer, but this ruling is not so strictly observed as that covering day and night yarning.

Finally we may consider old Bob Harris's statement of how it was understood by the Catawba of a generation ago that story-telling was intended to develop the mind, to make children think, to teach them the ways of life. It gave them, he says, something to think about; otherwise they would lack the means of developing their minds through the experiences recounted of others concerning human beings and animals.

EXPLANATION OF SYMBOLS FOR SOUNDS USED IN THE TEXTS.

Consonants

p, b. bilabial

t, d, alveolar dental

k, g, medial palatal

In the above series the surds and sonants are generally fully distinguishable from each other. When aspiration is as strong as it is following the corresponding English stops, it is so marked, *p'*, *t'*, *k'*.

s as in English.

r weak anterior palatal trill, similar to Spanish r, soft, the contact period not being distinguishable. In Catawba this sound is not confused with d.

tc affricative like English *ch* in *much.*

ts apical affricative, not a common sound.

m, n, as in English, when weakly aspirated so indicated, as *m', n'.*

ŋ palatal *n.*

' breath release or aspiration following stop or vowel.

' glottal stop, medium in strength.

h clear open breath.

Vowels

a, medium as in English *father.*

i, short open as *i* in English *pin.*

i·, short closed as English *ee.*

o, medium short, often confused with *a* and *α.*

o·, longer than the preceding with lip closure, sometimes heard as *u.*

ɔ as *o* in German *voll.* Not a common sound but occurring when -*owa* coalesces to -*ɔ. ǫ* same nasalized.

u, medium short, similar to *oo* in English *spoon.*

e, short open, similar to *e* in English *met.*

ǝ, short obscure open vowel.

α, short open, similar to English *u* in *sun.*

ą, ę, į, ǫ, ų, nazalized vowels.

Nasalization tends to lengthen vowels. When followed by the glottal stop they suffer shortening perceptibly. Syllables are occasionally recorded without either when so heard in dictation.

As noted also by Gatschet vowels tend to be short.

Stress accent, marked by ', is important. Syllables not accented are pronounced with the word preceding them.

⟩ denotes rhetorical lengthening of vowels, + denotes prolongation.

The symbol ' indicates a long, accented vowel.

Consonant groupings

tk	td	tb	tm	tn	tr	ts	—	—	—
—	gd	gb	—	gn	gr	—	—	—	—
pk	—	—	—	—	pr	ps	—	ptc	—
bk	—	—	—	—	br	bs	—	—	—
nk	nd	—	—	—	—	—	nt	ntc	—
—	—	kb	—	—	kr	ks	kt	ktc	kp
—	—	—	—	dn	dr	—	—	—	—
—	—	—	—	—	cr(?)	—	ct(?)	—	—
—	—	mb	—	mn	—	—	—	—	mp
sk	sd	—	—	sn	sr	—	st	stc	sp

The consonant groupings never exceed two members. Consonants are not lengthened and doubled. Any stop consonant can terminate a syllable, and stops and spirants can initiate a syllable. Clusters, however, begin but do not terminate a word. Acoustically the above groups are syncopated syllables composed of two consonants separated by an obscure vowel. They are frequently so written in the dictations, i. e., *pər = pr, sər = sr, tər = tr, sən = sn.* When rapid dictation was first taken down from Mrs. Owl, *tr* was frequently heard as English surd *th* and was so recorded until it could be resolved into *tr* — and even *tər*. Similarly *br* sounds like *vr*, bilabial *v + r*, and was so recorded under the same conditions of dictation by Mrs. Owl. Otherwise *v* is absent. It was included by Gatschet in his list of sounds. Historically then the consonant combinations with *r* are coalescences through the loss of intervening obscure vowel *(ə)* in colloquial utterance. The speakers who perform these contractions give value to the vocalic interval when clearer and slowed-up pronunciation is required. In the texts, however, I have not systematically attempted to normalize the syllable forms given, as they varied on this point. For instance, the same forms may be found written as they were heard in their context with or without the interconsonantic vowel, hence -*səre⁰* = -*sre⁰*, -*kəri'·'* = -*kri·'·'*, *senu⁰* = *snu⁰*.

Semi-vowel combinations with consonants

hw	ky	—	—	kw	ky	k'h,	kh
gw	gy	—	—	dw	dy	—	—
—	—	ph	—	sw	—	—	—
—	ny	—	—	tcw	—	—	—
—	ty	t'h	—				

In rapid utterance the *y* groupings approach in value palatized consonant forms, the *h* groupings aspirated forms, and the *w*

2

groupings labialized forms, with which they may be historically related in Siouan phonetic development.

Some aids to the reading and handling of the texts, though not intended to state phonetic laws as yet, are as follows.

The variability of vowel pronunciation does not dissolve with the accumulation of dictated material. They seem rather to show motility of *e* and *i* (*i·*), *α* and *ǝ*, *o* and *u* as coordinates in a series. Rhetorical variance may possibly be due to influence of surrounding sounds, too irregularly controlled by the living informants to permit construction of laws of use at the present time. Consequently variances will be found in recording, such as *wi·'pǝre*, (19.5) *we'bi·re*, *we'bǝre* "catch" (22.11); *mi·*, (25.6), *me* "only, self," and the like. For *yαp*, "tree, wood" Gatschet records *ya'p*, *yo'p*, and *ye'p*, as sounds that "permute or interchange among themselves."

Neither nasalization of vowels nor the frequency of the glottal catch can be ignored in Catawba, as did Gatschet, to render the pronunciation of isolated terms in the reading of the texts intelligible to native ears. I have experienced this difficulty during the process of checking up with my informants previously recorded forms, both my own and those of other recorders of Catawba.

Nasalization of consonants gives a series *nd*, in which either element, *n* or *d*, becomes so weak as to approach the mute, i. e., *dǝpę*" "one", or *nǝpe*". Also *mb*, *mp*, may be a strong labial, heard as *b*, preceded by nasalized vowel. Where *m* was audible it was indicated, accounting for variances *i̧'pi·*, *i'mpi·* "fire".

c (English sh) occurs in a few words, its rarity was noted by Gatschet.

χ, surd palatal spirant, was at first occasionally heard, and so written; but proved to be variant of *'k*. Gatschet recorded it as infrequent, but his examples were not intelligible when read to informants. (He gives *taχtcide*, "kindle up", in place of *wa''katci·de*.)

The glottal stop (voiceless) is indeed an important sound in Catawba. It seems to have been entirely ignored by Gatschet and underestimated by others who have added to the Catawba material. So frequent is the sound that I may have overlooked it perhaps more than I realized.

Sentence formation and the grouping of syllables into words are largely arbitrary, being based upon sense and meaning and pauses in pronunciation. Sentences in the translations correspond to those in the Indian text.

The spacing of word elements and articles in the texts is not made uniform. Irregularities follow the manner in which they were combined or separated by pauses in dictation and by accentuation.

Brackets, [ ], appearing in the interlinear translations are synonyms or explanations added to clarify meaning.

PART I

MYTHS AND TALES

1. U'gni, the Comet.

a. The Bad Woman Who Stole a Boy and Became a Comet (III).

ya	yį·tcaᵖ	deʳtcire.	yɛpasi'ha	ya'	kį·
Woman	person child	lost.	Person poor she	woman	the

hinų'rəre.	no weʳkitą'rəre.	kutci'n	pa'kpi'	ki·	mǫhotą're.
stole him.	Then cried come.	Bird	woodpecker the	in	came.

əni'	ya'	kį·	duksunu'wi·ere	kį·mǫ'səre.	kustą'
Then ·	woman the		ear metals [ear bobs]	asked for.	Corn bread

ki'ye	hitaᵖ	mobəro'həre	kustą'	kį·.	i'swątak
the	her breast	in put	corn bread	the.	River across

kutpi·	yį·tca	ka'nəre.	kustą'	kį· ną'həre	kustą'kį·
beyond	person child	find.	Corn bread the	ate	corn bread the

yį·tca'wa	kų'həre.	kustą'	kį· nąparąᵖhəre	yu'ksu
person child her	gave it.	Corn bread the	ate all up	his mother

ki·	mą'həre.	yį·tca'	kį·	duksu'gmǫtare
the	he knew it.	Person child the		back to the house in took

yuksu'	yapi'tę	mǫtukę'həre.	odapəda're
his mother	tree hollow [hollow log]	in put her.	Went hunting

wi·dəbo'ye hį· kowa're.	wi·ya	ki'	kai·həre	ki·tʿhəre	hi'tak
deer a he kill.	String	the	cut	it broke	on breast

bəro'həre	wi·dəbo'ye	kį·	nųwi'həre	nų'wi·ya	ki'tʿhəre.
when put on	deer	the	tied	tie string	broke.

yamusi'ka	ki'tʿhəre	yitʿki't'ha,	"apo' + apo' +
Woman old now	it broke	broke in pieces,	"Apo' + apo' +!

ta'ma hyu' + i·!"	mo'no	mǫhuktuikəre	"suknu
tama hyu' + i·!" [She cried]	ground	in on downfell,	"House my

wi·ʳrare."	yį̨tca	hį'	yuksu'	durukʿtcu'kʿhəre
burned down!"	Person child	a	his mother	back again took away

2*

yɛkɔrį́ʾhɔre.	*wi'ya*	*hukʿho"tcɔre*	*wi'ya*	*hukda"tcɔre*
people good.	String	down let	string	down make let

u'gni·	*huktu'khɔre*	*ki'*	*ya'musi·*	*ki·*	*huktu'kɔre*
u'gni· [comet]	down fell	the	woman old	the	down fell

wapitnu'tusaʾ	*huktu'kʿha*	*ya' kį·*	*bara'hɔre.*
star tailed [comet]	down fell she	woman the	bad.

yɛkɔrį́	*hi·mba'ri*	*mǫku'tcɔre.*	*ya' kį·*	*kuri'hi·nu namǫ́*
People good	heaven	in went.	Woman the	son small cloud

hɔrɔre	*ayɑ́bari'ʾhɔre*	*namǫ́ hatcu're.*	*yį·tca'na*
was [in] clear, pretty, blue sky	cloud very.	Person child my

kɔri'naʾ	*namǫ́hɔre.*
good son my	cloud is.

FREE TRANSLATION.

A woman lost her child. It was a poor woman who stole him. The mother went about crying. A bird, the woodpecker, came along, [and told the mother that he would give her some bread for her lost boy to eat and show her where he was hidden if she would give him her ear ornaments]. Then [the woodpecker] asked for her ear ornaments [and she gave them to him] and put the corn bread in the breast of her dress. Then she found her child across the river. She had eaten some of the corn bread herself, then she gave some of it to her child which he ate up greedily [as the woman who had stolen him was very poor and was starving him]. The stolen child knew it was his own mother [when she came and gave him the bread]. The child took his mother into the hut and concealed her in a hollow log. Then he went deer hunting and killed one. [He sent the woman who had stolen him to bring back the deer meat]. [In the meantime] he cut the packstrap in a number of places so that it broke when [the woman who had stolen him] put it on her breast when she had tied up the deer to carry it back. The tie-string broke, it broke in pieces for the old woman now, "Apo +! apo +! Tamahyu + i· +!" (Exclamations), she cried. The load fell on the ground. "My house is burned down," [she cried as she saw a smoke where the boy had set her hut on fire and ran home]. The boy then took his mother away with him to where the good people lived. [They rose in the air to the sky]. He let down a string as they rose and the old woman [as she took hold of it to go above with the boy and his mother] fell down. *Ugni* [the comet] fell down [through the sky] a tailed star, the bad woman fell down. The good people [the boy and his mother] went up to the "Where they never die" [Heaven], where the son is now a cloud in the clear blue sky. "My boy, my good son, is a cloud!" [she said].

b. The Eagle Kidnapper, the Pileated Woodpecker, U'gni the Comet, and the Sky Rope. (II).

we'ara'dre	*yamusi'*	*wi·təki⁰are.*	*witciktci·⁰*	*yintərɔ·'*
Long time ago	woman	old	potatoes dig.	Bald eagle	child

inu'yere.	*yamusi·⁰*	*kį·*	*mų'kip'ha*	*kəmara''hərе.*	*witciktci·⁰*
steal.	Woman	old	the	crazy	nearly.	Bald eagle

kį·	*kadumi're*	*mu'si·*	*ka*	*dugya'ne.*	*pakpi'-*
the	raise [him]	grown	now [before]	again got back.	Pileated

kəre	*ka'*	*hi·ne're*	*"kuri'ya'*	*dugda'nire*	*ugra'nere*
Woodpecker	a	told	"Son your	again I back [get]	wash[ing]

yantca'mǫntu⁰	*da'nire."*		*pakpe ki'*	*hį'here*
creek in	I saw."	Pileated	Woodpecker	the	who saw

yamusi'	*kį·.*	*hi·ku'hi·re*	*duksəni'*	*kį·*	*wi·ni't'*	*hinai're*
woman	old the.	He told her	earring	the	give	told [her]

"ye'ta	*hi·nai're*	*kuri'*	*ya'*	*tcip'ha'nire*	*hi·*	*nai're."*	*pakpe'-*
"You [I'll]	tell	son	your	where saw the	[I'll]	tell."	Pileated

kəre	*hi·ni·''ire*	*duksəni'*	*wi·ndo're.*	*"ha'wo'*	*naitco're*
Woodpecker	who told	earrings	give.	"Thanks	say much

kri·ndugda'nkį·ye¹	*namusa⁰tcore".*
son my back again the get	I glad much".

FREE TRANSLATION.

A long time ago an old woman went to dig potatoes. A bald eagle stole her child. The old woman was nearly crazy. The eagle raised him and he was grown before he got back. A pileated woodpecker told [the old woman that her son was back saying] "I saw your son washing in the creek. I will get him back again." The pileated woodpecker saw the old woman's [ear-rings]. He told her "If you will give me your ear-rings, I will tell you where your son is." The old woman gave the ear rings to the woodpecker who told [her where her son was]. [She said], "I am very thankful to get my son back again. I am very glad."

---

¹ Contraction of *kuri'na dugda'n kį·ye.*

1c. *The Eagle Kidnapper. Variant* (II).

Hi·mba'ri·we	*meu'tcere*	*wa'riwe.*		*hapmǫ"re*
Heaven,	alone there is	Never-Dies.	(God)	Up above go

maho'tcire	*hi·mba'ri*	*monamu'ᵕrere.*	*kuri'wa'*	*ni·nuha'prare*
go there	Heaven	world want go.	Son her	up go

na'pre	*ko'ᵕrere*	*ni·nuha'prare*	*wi·yaru'p*	*hukai"hare.*	*ume·'*
two	went	up go	rope	down hang.	Alone

Ugni'	*huktu'gere*	*wi'ya*	*ki't'here.*	"*huktu'ksere*
Ugni' (Comet)	down back [fall]	rope	break.	"Down fall I

naci·a'tcore,"	*kạ'uhatcore*	"*hopo'⟨*	*ha'na*
I am frightened,"	cry out much,	"[exclamation]	[you see]

kuda're	*hopo'⟨*	*naci·a a'tcore*	*dopora'p*
where I am going	[exclamation]	I am frightened much	some hurt

dantco're."	*yamusi'*	*ki·*	*we'tco're.*
I find much."	Woman	old	the cry much.

FREE TRANSLATIONS.

[All the people in the] world want to go up above to Heaven where God alone is. [A woman and] her son went up and left a rope hanging down [from the sky]. Ugni [the comet] took hold of the rope and tried to go up alone and the rope broke. [She] cried out, "I am falling down, I am frightened." "Hopo!" (Ex-ᵕclamation). "You see where I am going." "Hopo!" (exclamation). 'I find that I am badly hurt and I am very [badly] frightened." The old woman cried and cried.

2. *Origin of the Red Winged Blackbird and Dove.* (III).

kutci'n	*hawok'tce"*	*hitci'psəkạ're*	*itu'se*	*tạ'tukta're*	*tcụ'wi·*
Bird	black	wing red	dove	quarrel	bugs

kusa'wəha.	*ituse'ki·*	*tạtu'kha*	*emi'krure.*	*yamusi'ha*
about.	Dove the	quarreled	fought.	Old woman now

moho'	"*duwe'*	*tantca"*	*yetcu'wi· nǫ'suwe,*
there came,	"What	doing you?	I take you with me will,

do'pa'	*hiritpa"awe.*"	*ituse'*	*ka*	*kɔ'we*	*yamusi'⁾*
something	shoulder some may."	Dove	now	she killed	old woman.

kərį·hi'we.''	*kutci'n*	*kį· tų^ᵖ*	*kowa're*	*tu'gi·na-*
"Good she seems like."	Bird	the little	she killed	she ate it

parą^ᵖhəre.	*yamusi'*	*kį*	*ku'kawe*	*hitci'psəką'kį·.*
entirely.	Old woman	the	gave it may have	wings red the.

The black bird with wings red [Red-winged Blackbird] and the dove quarreled about insects. The dove quarreled and fought. An old woman now came along saying, "What about you? I will take you with me and something may be [put] on your shoulder" Now, the little old woman, she killed that dove. [She said], "She seems like a good person." She killed the little bird and ate it all up. The old woman evidently gave it its red wings.

3. How Pileated Woodpecker Got his Red Crest and Robin his Red Breast. (II).

pa'kpe	*ki·*	*kutci'n*	*agəre^ᵖ*	*uksəre'here*	*utka'nereko'*
Woodpecker	the	bird	other	look like was	long while ago.

wi·ya'ske'		*səką'*	*hiską^ᵖ*	*nųwi'here*	*yę təro'wa'krere.*
String red [ribbon]		red	his head	tie	child had.

yętərowa^ᵖ	*hiską^ᵖ*	*səką're.*	*huka't*	*pa'kpe*	*kį' ni·te'm hiską^ᵖ*
Child her	his head	red [was].	Now	woodpecker	the all head

səką're.	*ya'səse^ᵖ*	*wi'rą'tcure*	*ota^ᵖ*	*wi'rahį'we*	*kutci'n*
red [are].	Tree cut (brush)	burn much	he	burned got	bird

wi'rahi'we.	*wi'spakpa'k*	*hi·ta^ᵖ*	*səką're.*
burned got.	Robin	his breast	red is.

A long while ago, the woodpecker looked like the other birds. A child had a red ribbon on her head and she tied it on his head. And the woodpecker's head became red. Now the woodpeckers all have red heads.

The brush was burned and he, the bird, got burned. [The] robin got burned [and that is why] his breast is red.

4. How Yellow Hammer Got her White Inner Wings. (II).

watca'k	*tcina'*	*i'swą'*	*ya'ktca*	*kuna'nire*	*i·swą^ᵖ*	*təri'ksere.*
Flicker	shake	river	cross branch	try	river	wade.

yatatcu'ntare	wi'dyo	di'gdaha	na'mani·	digda're.
Across coming	meat	on back carry	bundle	on back.

nunta'ktce	ha'kpanare	hani·kį'	kata'ktci·re
Covering white	inside [was]	this how the	now white is

nunisi'wą'	ha'kɔpaɔ	hitcipi'n	ta'ktcire.
blanket	inside	wing	white.

FREE TRANSLATION.

The flicker was trying to wade across the river. And he was coming across carrying a bundle of meat on his back. It was covered with a white blanket [inside his wings] and that is how the inside of his wings became white.

5. *How the Wolf was Frightened and Became Wild.* (II).

tasi·su'rieɔ	ną'pri·	i·ro're nɔpę̨ɔ	tciri'kᶜhare,	"naci·a'-
Dog wild (wolf) two	went	one	ran away,	"I am frightened

tcore	sa'wana	tcuwi'	ha'aų're."	nɔpe'ra	ki'ye	hi·yoha're,
much	Shawnee	many	are coming."	One and	the	forbid,

naci·atco're	udyi·tce".	wari'kᶜhade!	sa'wana
"I am frightened much,	say don't.	Hush!	Shawnee

yę mbara'tcure."	ipake'	kį· hapko"ere yaphapko"ere	do'pa
people bad much."	Partridge the	up fly tree up fly	something

yu'yaretcure.	tą'si·su'rieɔ	deme'tcęb.
noise rolling much.	Wolf	alone there.

tą'si·surieɔ	ya'phakɔpa	na'te	wǫ̨ᶜwǫ̨ᶜstere.	"ta'ntci·	webia're
Wolf	tree under	then	howl.	"Can not	I catch

pi'kat kę'hareare."	ka't	hi·mi·para'ɔantare.
fly far away."	Indeed,	who alone completely gone.

tą'si·surie'	mǫtce".
Wolf	wild.

FREE TRANSLATION.

Two wolves were going along and one ran away [saying], "I am much frightened, many Shawnee are coming." The one with him told him to stop saying, "I am frightened much. Don't say that, Hush! The Shawnee are very bad." The partridges flew up, flew up a tree like something rolling heavily. The wolf was alone there. The wolf then howled under the tree. "I cannot catch them [the partridges] they fly far away." Indeed, he was left completely alone when they went. [That is why the] wolf [is] wild.

6. *How Opossum Lost his Bushy Tail.* (II).

"deme′hetcę	*hitci′p*	*mba′resa′⟨sa."*	*dəpətustrę″*	*ku′tere*
"I alone here	who top	pretty tail."	Opossum[1]	say

"pą′yątus	*wį·″here."*	*haktco′ką tuktca′re*	*tərą′ntcure.*
"Squirrel tail	like."	Hole now in he went	when out so [come].

"watku′t di·tusisi″	*para″here.*	*unia′t⸳ dika′k*	*diksito′parą″sere*
"Snail my tail hair finished.	Then my body	my back turn I [did]

ditusisi″	*paį″hare."*	*yare′mitco′re*	*duktcowa′*
my tail hair	no more."	Ashamed much	back come not

mo′nu da′panire.	*hi′ską⸳*	*haksera′*	*utko′re*	*ya′remi hitcə-*
year one.	His head	down low	turn	ashamed who

paso″hatcu′re.
slobber fluid much.

The opossum said, "I alone have a tail with a pretty top. It is like the squirrel's tail." He went in his hole and came out [saying] "The snail has finished [eaten off] my tail hair. Then my body, my back I turned and my tail hair was not there." He was very much ashamed and did not come out for one year. His head was low and "He-who-slobbers-fluid-much", (opossum) turned away ashamed.

7. *How Tree Frog Taught Toad to Cry.* (II.)

dəpətci′kpo	*kį·*	*ya′kətci·*	*wa′rəre*	*hi·saretcu′re*
Ancient [who] steps (toad)	the	woman spouse	die	who sorry very

we″hərə	*ka′here*	*ta′ntci·we⸳ha′re.*	*wa′rarə⸳*	*kį· hi·nkui′re*
cry	try	could not cry.	Tree frog	the who told

"hi·nai′wi·	*wei·ki′*	*nawati′we.*	*ni·sa′renaitcui′re!"*
"[I] tell you	cry the	I teach you,	I sorry say very!"

we″ta⸳ta″hewe	*kąuhatco′re.*
cry ta' ta' may	weep much.

---
[1] Literally "Ancient-One-tail-clear (pale)."

FREE TRANSLATION.

The toad's wife died and he was very sorry. He tried to cry but
he could not. The tree frog told the toad, "I will teach yow how to
cry. Say, 'I am very sorry,' then you may cry and weep (mourn)
much," [the tree frog said].

8. *How Chipmunk Got his Stripes.* (II).

də' pəndataksoso"			*nɑ̨' prəri*	*tumo"*
One [who] back pretty (chipmunk)			two [were]	acorns

atku" hruwe	*kaktcu'*	*ntu' gbako' re*	*we' ra*	*ki·*	*wi·hirɑ̨' we*	*u' nti·*
gather going	hole	then in put	winter	the	eat some	bag

ditugbaka' re.	*we"ru*	*ka' ktcu*	*tugbaka' re.*	*"dasui' stere,*	*tcirikste' re*
in put.	Winter	hole	in put.	"Play I do,	run I do

tumǫ'	*a' tkowa*	*de' ra*	*tuko' tcere.*	*kaka' sənapara""*
acorn	gather	my and	back itches.	Scratch, thoroughly me!"

ure' re	*kutere*	*kakasənapara"*	*sunta' re*	*ndatuko'*	*kuri"tcure.*
True	said is	scratch completely	went	then back	pretty very is.

FREE TRANSLATION

Two chipmunks were going to gather acorns in a bag and put
them in a hole. They would put them in a hole and in the winter
they would eat some. One said, "I play, I run and gather acorns
and my back itches. Scratch me thoroughly." It is said to be true
that he scratched his back so thoroughly that it left marks which
make it look very pretty.

RABBIT TALES

9a. *Rabbit Steals the Fire from the Buzzards.* (II)

utka' nihere	*i·səne"*	*į'mpi'*	*ba' t'here.*	*i'səne"*	*ba' gre*	*tci·hi'*
Long time ago	buzzard	fire	keep back.	Buzzard	around	cold

wa"here	*hi·tci'p*	*di·ta"are.*	*dəpəhwa"*	*ki̧·*	*į'mpi*	*wi·ni·pa'*	*wi-*
sit	wing	open.	Rabbit	the	fire	his foot	warm

kintcu' re	*haka' t·e,*	*"ni·pa"*	*tci'"tcure*	*ni'pa'*
[want] much	now indeed,	"My foot	cold much	my foot

pɑ̨' tcure."	*"wa' hare*	*ye' ka*	*taį' tciki̧' hare."*	*hu' gdu-*
near fire much."	"No!	you	you cannot [do it]."	Around

*ki'here   hapitko'ra,   "hakpi   ni'ntcade   ndo'wa   taptaptcera*ᵖ-
back again   behind came,   "Help   me   for I   frozen

*wehere."   o'ta*ᵓ   *wataptco're.   dəpę́   i'sәne*ᵓ   *hisa'rare   hitcip*ᶜ*ha'*-
nearly."   He frozen nearly.   One buzzard   who sorry   his wing

*brere   dəpəhwą́   kį·   yap   itcәwesi'sį·   hį́'pi·*ᶜ*ta   aso'-*
raised up   rabbit   the   wood   pine splinters   his toes   between

*sapsa'phere   hi'pi·   mǫtcu're.   i'mpi*ᵓ   *hǫwakatcu're.   į'mpi·   kį́'*
put [them]   his toe   sing much.   Fire   blazed much.   Fire the

*hrere   ya'p   kį·   wa'khere   dəpəhwą́   kį·   tci'rik*ᶜ*hatcu're   wikintcu're*
go to wood   the blaze   rabbit   the   run   much   hot very

*kate*ᵖ   *yapawą́'mǫhere   dabwo'hahaure   ka't·e*ᵓ
indeed   jump up and down singing   through woods come   indeed

*į'mpi·tcuri're.   "dəpəhwą́   ki·   kurį·*ᵖ*here.   i'mpi·   patkį·   kadwi'kaure.*
fire much.   "Rabbit   the good is.   Fire big   now warm come.

*yę́'nite'mp   wą́'nt*ᶜ*hode   hi·yara'we."*
People all   sit down come   may get warm."

Free Translation.

A long time ago the buzzard kept the fire back. It was cold and
the buzzards all sat [around the fire with their] wings outspread.
The rabbit was very cold indeed and he asked if he could warm
his foot. [He said,] "My foot is very cold. My foot I must put by
the fire." [The buzzard said,] "No, you cannot do it." [The rabbit
went away and] came around behind them again [and said,] "Help
me, for I am nearly frozen." He was nearly frozen. One buzzard
who [felt] sorry for him raised up his wing and the rabbit put
pine splinters between his toes, singing all the time. [He went
under his wing and lighted them.] The pine splinters blazed up.
The fire got into wood. The rabbit ran off because the fire [that he
was carrying] was very hot. He came through the woods jumping
up and down singing. "The rabbit is good. The fire is big and warm
now and all people may come sit down and get warm."

9b. *Rabbit Steals Fire from the Buzzards* (III).

*isәne*ᵖ   *į'pi   bat*ᶜ*hәre.   dəpəhwą́'pą́'sę   itciwe*ᵖ   *sęsę*ᵖ*hәre*
Buzzard   fire   hold back.   Rabbit belly-old[1]   pine   splints

---

[1] The usual name for rabbit, *dəpəhwą́*ᵖ means "one jumps or sits". The
term *pą́'se*, "Belly-old" is one way of referring to rabbit and is locally
rendered as "Old Rabbit", while another term *pąwą́*ᵖ "belly or foot jumps
or sits", is given as a short form.

hi·pa^⁰as   *kip‘ki′p‘ᵊre.*   "*nį·pa’*   *tci^⁰hᵊre*"   "*į′pɪ*
his foot bottom   stick in.   "My foot cold," [said rabbit].   "Fire

atcį′rikwᶐ   *hade.*"   *hi′pa’*   *wɔ′kᵊre*   *ya′psᵊtas*
a little closer sit   do."   His foot take fire   wood cut made (prairie)

wɔ′kᵊre   *kį′hᵉ^ᵊ*   *i′pa*   *hara′hᵊre.*
take fire   close he   foot   warms.

Free Translation.

The Buzzard held back the fire. The rabbit, "Belly-old", stuck
pine splinters in the bottom of his foot. [The rabbit said] "My
foot is cold." "Do sit a little closer to the fire," [said the buzzard].
[The splinters in] his foot caught fire and set the prairie on fire.
[He was so] close [to the fire he got his] foot warm.

10. Rabbit Steals Water from the Snapping Turtle (II)

kaya′skᶐtᵊro   *yᶐhi·*   *ye′kį·*   *ba′t‘here.*
Turtle head big (snapping turtle)   water   the   keep back.

yᶐtci·   *kį′*   *sukhɔ′*   *wᶐre*   *ba′t‘here.*
Water branch (spring)   the   over (covered)   sit   keep back.

kaya′skᶐtᵊro   *mba′ratcure*   *otɑ^ᵊ*   *ome′bat‘here.*
Turtle head big   bad much   he   alone keep back.

dᵊpᵊhwᶐ′   *kį·*   *oku′mara′re.*   "*de′ta*   *ye′kį·*   *namu^ᵊere*
Rabbit   the   came up with him.   "I   water the   want

yehi′ye′   *pagye′ra atcu′re.*"   "*yetɑ′ntci·wa′re.*"   *kaya′-*
water some   need much."   "Water cannot [have]."   Snapping

skᶐtᵊro′   *kį·*   *hi′yohare.*   "*mi′nin*   *kru′ksᵊre*   *ha′wo′nai′re*"
turtle the   forbid.   "Give me   I drink   [I′ll] say, "Thank you!"

kaya′skᶐtᵊro′ki·   *hi′yoha′re.*   *mᶐtui′re*
Turtle head big the (snapping turtle)   refused.   meanwhile

dᵊpᵊhwᶐ′ kį·   *mo′na*   *pa‘sore ka′ya’*   *hakapɑ^ᵊ*   *kį·kį′hare yehi·ye′*
rabbit   the   ground   scratch turtle   underneath   ditch   water

tciri′k‘here.   *tci′rik*   *hatcu′re*   *mo′na*   *ni·tɑ^ᵊhare*   *yᶐ^ᵊtca′-*
run.   Run   much so   earth   all over [was]   water branch

haktco′   *yehiyᵉ′*   *sᶐ′ntakuri^ᵊtcure.*
hole.   Water   flows well much.

FREE TRANSLATION.

The turtle-with-the-big-head (snapping turtle) kept back the water [from the people]. He sat over the spring and kept the water back. The snapping turtle was very bad. He alone kept the water back. The rabbit came up to him and said, "I want the water. Some water [I] need very much." "[You] cannot have the water", [said] the snapping turtle. [If you] give me a drink I'll say, "Thank you." The snapping turtle refused. ⸰In the meanwhile the rabbit scratched the ground underneath the turtle [and made a] ditch [and the] water ran [out]. So much ran out all over the earth that it made gullies. The water flowed very well [since that time]. (Explains reason why water flows now).

11. Rabbit and Snail Go for a Doctor. (I)

dəpəhwą'	*hįⁿ*	*watku't*	*hįꜣ*	*hęⁿ*	*yę*	*da'kta*	*i·na'hę'.*	*dəpəhwą*
Rabbit	a	snail	a		person	doctor	go for.	Rabbit

kįⁿ	*kora'hahe'.*	*dəpəhwą'*	*kį·t*	*dugho'yat*	*watku't*	*kįt*
the	went right on.	Rabbit	the	back came	snail	the

su'nti·	*hapiⁿ*	*sakową'he'.*	*watku't*	*kį*	*dugho'mątu't‘,*
door	step	on top sat.	Snail	the	back came when [said],

"*da'kta*	*hone'?*"	"*ha'gwani·hęⁿ!*	*da'kta*	*ha*	*hyęⁿ.*[1]	*yę'*
"Doctor	come did he?"	"Yes, he did!	Doctor	did	come.[1]	Person

ware sa	*kį·t‘*	*wa'resawe*	*nu'nti·*	*ną'pri*	*hęⁿ.*"
sick	the	dead	moon	two."	

FREE TRANSLATION.

A rabbit and a snail went for a doctor. The rabbit went straight on. When he returned he found the snail sitting on the door step. When the snail came back he asked, "Did the doctor come?" "Yes he did! The doctor came.[1] The sick person has been dead for two months," was the answer.

TERRAPIN TALES.

12. How Terrapin Married Chief's Daughter and Made an Ice House. (II)

kayaⁿ	*ya*	*akpi'no.*	*yę'*	*mi·ra*	*kį'*	*nowa'*
Terrapin	woman	marry.	Man	great (chief)	the	daughter

---

[1] The ensuing passage was added by Mrs. Owl's husband who had heard it while living on the Catawba reservation. Mrs. Owl then furnished the translation. A similar tale is common among the Virginia Powhatan.

akpi·'no. dukha hę́ ⟨saᵖware   *kaskąteroᵖhiʾ*
marry.   Back long time ago   terrapin head big (snapper) and the

      kaįhi'nohiᵖ   *kaya'tci·reʾ*
terrapin small (box tortoise) and the   turtle small (mud turtle)

hįᵖ   *kasəmiᵖ*   *hiʾ*   *raᵖhere.*   *yę́mi·ra'*
and the   turtle smell (stink turtle) and the   together.   Chief

kį·   *nowa'*   *hi·ma'retcure.*   *ni·te'm*   *hi·wi·ni'*   *i·mu'rehę̆ʾ.*
the   daughter his   sleep much.   All   who marry   want did.

ni·te'm   *koᶜhrere*   *yąsudeᵖare*   *kųᵖ*   *bayiᵖre*   *ų́mbaniᵖ*   *tco'ware*
   All   run   road side of   slow   go   go slow   much

kąu'hatcure   *do'potci'kanehi·'we.*   *dəpę́*   *tci·ka*   *mara're*   *ume'*
cry out much   something wrong like.   One   there   arrive   alone

mara're.   *kayaᵖ*   *yę́mi·ra*   *kį·*   *nowa'*   *akpi'no*   *hi·tca'wa*
arrives.   Terrapin   chief   the   daughter   marry   night

sukərę́   *eka'tcere.*   *su'k himbaretcui're*   *mǫ'hi·*   *suk*
house fine   caused to build.   House nice much   ice   house

ka'tcere.   *ya'kitcaʾ*   *dumara're.*   *hitca'wa*   *ki·*   *uksotco're*
built.   Woman wife   took there.   Night   the   rain much

mǫ'hi·tci·   *paraᵖhere.*   *hitca'wa*   *kį*   *təra'ŋkupe*   *yaʾhere*
ice there   completely melt.   Night   the   outside lie down   were

su'kopaį̇·'hare.   *su'gwa*   *watərąᵖ*   *parąᵖhere*   *uni're*   *ku'təre.*
house none was.   House his   wash away   completely   so   he says.

FREE TRANSLTAION.

The terrapin married a woman. He married the chief's daughter.
Back a long time ago the terrapin-with-the-big-head [the snapping
turtle][1] the small terrapin [box tortoise][2] and the small turtle
[mud turtle][3] and the turtle that smells [stink turtle][4] were all
together. The chief and his daughter were asleep. All [of them]
want[ed] to marry [her]. They all ran along the roadside going
slowly, slowly and crying out as though something was wrong.
One of them arrived there alone. The terrapin married the chief's

---

[1] Chelydra serpentina.
[2] Cistudo Carolina.
[3] Cinosternum Pennsylvanicum.
[4] Cromochelys odoratus.

daughter that night and build a fine house. [He] built a nice house of ice. The woman, his wife, he took there. During the night it rained so much that the ice completely melted. [They were] lying outside at night [because there] wasn't any house. His house was washed away completely, so he said.

13. *Race between Deer and Terrapin.* (I)

wi·debo' ye	*hį·*	*kayaᵖra*	*ukantceᵖtiri·eᵋ'*	*tci'rikᶜha*
Deer	the	Terrapin	with going race it is said	run

utkeraᵖ	*unia' tᶜ*	*kosaᵖha*	*"taiyedoᵖ"'*	*uniatᶜ*
certain distance.	Then	stop,	"Where are you?"	Then

kaya	*kįnt*	*"ha'nitci·'rire"'*	*uniatᶜ*	*hatatkoᵖwǫᵖ*	*"ha'nitci·rie."*
Terrapin	the,	"Here me!"	Then	in front sat,	"Here me!"

widebo'ye	*kį·t*	*du'gǝra·haᵓ*	*tci·ri'kᶜhatiri·eᵓ*	*burukᶜ*	*kusa'-*
Deer	the	again	run it is said	again back	stop

hati'rie.	*unia't ᶜ*	*"taiyeniᶜ'"*	*hatatkoᵖ*	*wǫᵖ*	*hani'*	*"hani-*
it is said.	Then	"Where are you?"	in front	sit	here,	"Here

tci'rie"	*kaya'*	*kį't*	*hadu'tatirieᵖ*	*kaya'*	*kį·t*	*mi·raᶜhati'rie.*
me!"	Terrapin	the	said it is said.	Terrapin	the	excelled it is said.

FREE TRANSLATION.

A deer and a terrapin were going to race together, it was said. They ran a certain distance then stopped. "Where are you?" [said the deer]. Then the terrapin said "Here I am!" Then there in front of him [the deer] he sat. "Here I am!" The deer ran again, it is said, and back again and stopped, it is said. Then [he called] "Where are you?" In front of him sat [the terrapin]. "Here I am!" the terrapin is said to have cried. The terrapin excelled him, it is said.

14. *Recitative from story of Bull Frog, Terrapin and Snail go to Bring Doctor Toad.* (IV)

Yuᵖmi·	*taᵖna*
I start to go somewhere	

tcintu'	*pǝrǫ'de*
sliding	roll

wǫ'nkį	*ya's*	*datkohi'*
Going	again	up yonder

suktci'pki·   *ha't'kut'*
hill top   down hill

da'pą' *arą"araį'*
pond   bull-frog

ya'mukwą ha   *tcikų`.*
in water jump   splash!

Note. — The above is a recitation in verse, representing some notion of meter in the Catawba ear. It is to be repeated rapidly in a sing-song tone, the measures appearing as follows: —

$$
\begin{array}{ll}
\text{\char'40} - & \text{\char'40} - \\
\smile \text{\char'40} & \smile \text{\char'40} \smile \\
\text{\char'40} \smile - & \smile \smile \text{\char'40} \\
\smile \text{\char'40} - & \text{\char'40} - \\
\text{\char'40} - & \smile \text{\char'40} \smile \text{\char'40} \\
\text{\char'40} \smile \text{\char'40} \smile & \smile \text{\char'40}
\end{array}
$$

The word form is so mutilated to conform to some scheme of rhythm that the translation is only a rough one.

Bull-Frog, Terrapin and Snail go to bring Doctor Toad (IV).

The story of a bull-frog and a terrapin who were sent to get the toad who was a medicine man. The frog jumped so fast that he arrived before the terrapin had gotten more than part way. And the terrapin felt so ashamed that he went back home. The next time they sent the snail to get the medicine man, but the snail was so slow that he never got beyond the door-step. Someone made a complaint against him, so he too felt ashamed. Finally the terrapin and bull-frog were again sent to bring the toad doctor. This time the terrapin took the toad on his back and brought him so promptly that the bull-frog was left behind. He was so ashamed that he jumped into the pond — *tcikų`*! "ker-plunk!" and has lived there ever since.

15. Logger-Head Terrapin, the Snake and the Man. (III)

ara't'kanire   *yę* *yį·bəritca"* *dəpəda'*   *i'swątak.*
Long time ago   Indian   man   hunting went   across river.

unia't *ka'ya* *ya' hį·* *ewi·tkərų'* *unia't* *į'ti* *ya' kį·*
Then   terrapin   snake the   fight with.   Then   on rock   snake the

itcika' *o'watca'* *yę'* *mą*   *da*   *mǫtu"* *ki'həre.*   *ya patkį'*
how   using   man   coming went   when   shot him.   Snake big

ha	*i̯'ti·*	*mǫ'həre.*	*kǫ*	*wota're,*	*kǫwo-*
now	from rock	came out.	He	cried out,	cried out for someone

na'ire	*yəma'yi·*	*mǫ'hare.*	*"mosa'pəde*	*dukho'wade!"*
to come	boat	ask for.	"Hurry do	brink it back here!"

ya'	*ki̯·*	*yę'ye*	*hę'*	*kowa're*	*nǫ'wi·həre.*	*i'swǫtak*
Snake	the	man	the	killed	tied [coiled about] him.	Across river

ka patki̯'	*kusa"*	*ka pa'tki̯·*	*ki·ye*	*katuke'həre.*	*yę'ye*
hole big	standing there	hole big	the	hole in put.	Indians

kəre	*i·sa'retcure*	*i'swǫtak*	*wǫ'ye*	*we"ki·ye.*	*i'swǫ*	*hugda're*
these	sorry very	across river	sitting	crying.	River	fell

mǫtu'	*i·ya'nəre*	*no'suk*	*ha'kəpare*	*ya'*	*ki̯·*	*i·t'pak*
when	found him	arm	under	snake	the	blood flowing

kamǫ'təre.
sucked it.

FREE TRANSLATION.

A long time ago an Indian man went hunting across the river. Then terrapin [there] was fighting with a snake. Then when a man came there using a bow he shot the snake on a rock. The big snake came out from the rock. He [the man] cried out, called out for someone to come, asking for a boat. "Hurry up, bring it here!" The snake killed the man by coiling about him. Across the river a big hole (cave) was visible and [the snake] put him in there. The Indians felt badly sitting crying on the opposite bank. When the river fell they found him, from under his arm the snake had sucked the blood.

MISCELLANEOUS TALES.

16. Opossum Tricks the Deer and the Wolves. (III)

dəpətustre"	*ki̯·*	*wɔ"*	*ki̯·*	*mǫtu'*	*ko'ʿhrere.*
(Opossum) One-tail-clear [of-hair]	the	snow	the	in	go.

ədrę' su	*puka'nire.*	*dəpətustrę"*	*"deme hatce'nǫ sa'sa.*
Persimmon tree	find.	Opossum [sings]	"I by myself here I.

ədrę'wi·	*tcǫ'we."*	*pa'səm*	*ki̯·*	*ədrę"wi*	*nǫ'dja.*	*wi·dəbo'ye*
Persimmon eat may."		Opossum	the	persimmons	eat.	Deer

ko'ware.	*wi·dəbo'ye*	*ki̯·*	*su'k*	*ki̯·*	*mǫtu"*	*hakwa're.*	*yap kida'*
came up.	Deer	the	hill	the	in	him[self] kill.	Tree up

3

ya'p kį· bo'həre ya'hakowa're. dəpətustrę⁰ kį·   ədrę́   wa'sap
tree the butt   him kill.   Opossum the persimmon basket

ti bu'gəre.   yaphi·tce're   mo'nuki'pəre.   tąsi su're kį·
the put.   Wood sharp   in ground stick.   Dog wild [wolf] the

ha'ure.   "ədrę   tą'tci yəpana'nəne?" "ya'p kį· hap kwą'hade
come. "Persimmon how   you get?"   "Tree the up jump do

ədrę⁰   pana're."   eni   tąsisu're   yap   uktu'kha   hakwa're.
persimmon get."   Then   wolf   stick   fall   him kill.

"deme'hətcena sa'sa"   "yəme'hatce're?" "det⁽ demehatce'na."
[Sings] "I myself here I."   "You alone here?"   "I   myself here I."

tąsi su're kį· dəpa'⁽həre "mǫsatcu're   ye'te   tai'yə   do'pə
   Wolf the   met, "Glad I very you where you something get

ni'yanə yę'na dəpę⁰ de'ntcəno" wi·k hade   bara'tcure kəde
is it not man my one   I lose."   Hush do bad very truly indeed

sa'wane   haha'ure   wirik⁽hadeha   nacia're."   tcirik⁽həre
partridges   come   quiet be   I am frightened."   Ran away

wa'sap   kai'here.   yap ha'p tca're. tąsisu're ki· hap⁽watcu're.
basket down [threw]. Tree up climb. Wolf the up jump much.

dəpətustrę' kį·   hapową⁰   hitcəpaso'tcure.   tą'sisu're
Opossum the up [tree sit]   his slobber froth much.   Wolf

ndo'tatcu're.   pa'səm ki· yap⁽hap⁽daretcu're   hįda'   kį·
chase him much. Opossum the tree up go much. Shadow   the

wo'ną.   yamukwą'ha   yap⁽ha' səmapą⁰ha. tci'rikha yap⁽ha'p-
like bite in water jump tree leaves mouth full.   Run   tree up

da're ka'dətugda're.   isəne' kį· yap⁽ha'pdareha. itu'se ha'p dane
go now hole in go. Buzzard the tree up go. Hawk up go

watku't hap⁽ke'ną.   "tą' yətciha'p⁽dane?"   dəpətustrę⁰   kį·
snail   up.   "How   you up get?"   Opossum   the

yarəmi·tcu'na. watku't⁽ kį· hitu's   so⁰ha.
ashamed very. Snail the his tail trimmed [by eating the hair].

yupi· səre't⁽   hate ki'datuke'həre.   pa'səm kį· we⁽stewe
Vehicle slide [sled] the on top in put. Opossum the cry

we⁽satcu're.   "ni·wɔ'de!"   "įpi'sere   ni·we'.   mǫtu'   dade
cry hard.   "Kill him!" "Fire this kill may. [Put] in   do

i·swą́ sere.''   *''yupi·sɘre′t'ha*   *debo′tugo′ wahade′.''*   *tciri′k*
river this.''   ''Sled [vehicle slide] the   thicket in take do.''   Ran

ha   *dugwe′ tame*   *we!*   *mi·a′ we.*   *a′ tɘhani′hɘre.*
off   back home always   [his] town   been.   That finish.

FREE TRANSLATION.

The opossum, ''One-tail-clear-of-hair'', went out in the snow.
[He] found a persimmon tree. The opossum [sang to himself] ''Here
I am by myself. I may eat persimmons.'' The opossum ate the
persimmons. The deer came up the hill and killed himself. [He
saw the opossum] up the tree and butted the tree and it killed
him [the deer]. Opossum put the persimmons in the basket. [Then
he took a piece of] sharp wood [and] stuck [it] in [the] ground. The
wolf came. [Said he] ''How do you get persimmons ?'' [Opossum
said,] ''you jump up the tree to get persimmons.'' Then the wolf
fell on the stick and was killed. [Opossum singing to himself said,]
''I am here by myself. I am.'' ''You alone here ?'' The wolf said.
''I am here by myself, I am,'' said the opossum. Then he met a
wolf. [The wolf said,] ''I am very glad to meet you. You have
something there, where did you get it ? Is it not the one man I
lost ?'' [Opossum said,] ''Hush, do be quiet. It is very bad indeed,
the partridges[1] will come. I am frightened.'' Opossum threw down
his basket and ran away. He climbed up a tree. The wolf tried
to jump up. Opossum sat up in the tree slobbering. He came down
and the wolf chased him. Opossum went up a tree. The wolf saw
his shadow in the water and jumped in but he only got his mouth
full of leaves. Opossum ran up the tree and went in his hole. The
buzzard went up, the hawk went up, [and the] snail [went] up.
Opossum said, ''How did you get up ?'' Opossum was very much
ashamed. The snail trimmed his tail [by eating the hair]. They put
him on a sled [vehicle slide]. Opossum cried. He cried hard.
[Some said]. ''Kill him.'' Some said, ''Put him in the fire, this fire
may kill him; or put him in this river.'' [Others said], ''Put him on
a sled and take him into the thicket.'' Opossum ran off back home
[to the thicket] which had always been his town. That's the finish.

17· *The Deer and the Sleeping Hunter.* (III)

napaᵖna′ wi·dɘbo′ye da′para′re.   *ataᵖ hugnapi! na′mɘre*   *ya*
Hunter   deer   hunt went.   He   down lay want   path

---

[1] Partridges become in folk-lore a figurative reference to enemies; the
Shawnee.

3*

mǫtu". wi·dǝbo' ye niakia' tere otα° hi'mbαre. hi'mαkupe're omę' kupe
in.   Deer   pass by   he   sleep.   Sleep lying alone lying

hi'mbαre   namα'p   nia'wo'here   wi·dǝbo' ye ki'   kųwo'hǝre.
sleep   sleep until   pass him   deer   the   pass by fast.

"yaphasku'   hi'wo   yę'ye   hi'wo   tαmahi°o⟨   naciatco're."
"Tree stump maybe man maybe [exclamation] I fear much."

FREE TRANSLATION.

A hunter went out to hunt deer. He lay down in the path. The deer passed by when he was asleep. He was asleep, lying alone asleep, sleeping until the deer passed by him going fast. The deer said, "Maybe it is a tree stump, maybe it is a man, *tαmahi'°o⟨,* I am afraid."

18. Deer Jumps across Catawba River. (II)

ya'   ki'   yi·tcα°here   yi·tcα°kawα'rǝre   o'ta ka'nire
Woman the   fishing   fishing the now sitting   she   saw

wi·dǝboy'e i'swα° yata' wα°hǝre wi·de·e° nuntera a're wα'hǝre.
deer   river across jump deer calf small with jump.

FREE TRANSLATION

A woman was fishing. Sitting there fishing, she saw a deer jump across [the] river, a small fawn jumped with [it].

19. Fox and Raccoon. (III)

tcigne' tǝpǝya'muye itǝpa°e.   "tcǝpǝtca°   do'pa
Raccoon   fox   met together.   "Somewhere something

tcαwe."   "ye'ka,   tcigǝne' ki·, "mi·ra°su'we."
we eat will." "You, [said] raccoon the, outdo I can."

tǝpǝya'muye hi·   "o'ka mi·ra°su'we."   da°   aha'
Fox   the [said], "Him outdo I can."   He went goose

wi'pǝre.   tǝ'pǝ tcigǝne' ki·t° yaremi're.   ya'remikida'-
caught.   Terrible raccoon the was ashamed. So ashamed he

hǝre.   "ye'ta hi·sa'rǝre."   aha' ki· hiskα° kų'rǝre,
lay down. "You I am sorry for." Goose the head he gave him,

tcigǝne' ki· nα'rǝre.
raccoon the ate it.

Raccoon and fox met together. "We will get something to eat somewhere," [said they]. "You," [said] the raccoon, "I can outdo." The fox [said], "I can outdo him." He went off and caught a goose. The terrible raccoon was ashamed, so ashamed that he lay down. "I am sorry for you," [said fox]. He gave him the goose head and the raccoon ate it.

20. Hawk and Buzzard. (III)

do'pa	*hi·nu'yeta'*	*itu'si·*	*ki·ye.*	*i·sɘnę*,		"*taįtci·-*
Something	steals	hawk	the.	Buzzard [said to],		"How

wayi'	*katcɘne'."*		*i·sɘne'*	*ki·*	*uta*ᵖ	"*warɘwe'*	*ki·*
living	make do you?"		Buzzard	the	said,	"Never dies	[God] the

ha'ksɘre."	*ɑn*	*itu'si*	*ki·*	"*yu*ᶜ	*yarɑ'daretcu're*
I wait for."	Then	hawk	the,	"yuᶜ	you will be very hungry

	det	*ni·yanido'!"*	*pi'kᶜhɘre*	*wi·tkɑ'*	*ki·*	*wi'pᶜhɘre.*
[always].		Me	see what I do!"	He flew off	chicken	the	caught.

hakowar'e	*i·sɘne'*	*ki·*	*nɑpɘrɑ'hɘre.*	"*wa'rɘwe*
He was killed.	Buzzard	the	at him up completely.	"God

haga'we	*hagakɘba'reho'we."*
wait on if,	wait on better will."

The hawk steals things. He said to the buzzard, "How do you make your living?" The buzzard said, "I wait for God [to take care of me]." Then said the hawk, "Oh! you will always be hungry. Me, see what I do." He flew off to catch a chicken, and was killed. The buzzard ate him up completely. "If one waits for God, one will wait for the better."

21. Buzzard Steals Fish. (II)

yęmusi'	*ki'*	*yi·tcɑ*ᵖ	*harare.*	*i·sɘne*	*ki'*	*yi*ᵖ	*ki·*	*hi·nu'yere*
Man	old	the	fishing	went.	Buzzard	the	fish	the	who steal

*dɘpę*ᵖ	*kuru'kᶜhare*	*ni·te'm*	*dukᶜha'rare*	*yęmusi'*	*ki'*	*yi*	*ki'*
one	swallow	all	home carry	man old	the	fish the

ni·te'm inde'ᶜtcere.	*i·sɘne*	*ki'*	*ni·te'm dotciri'kᶜhere.*
all	lose.	Buzzard	the	all	take run off.

An old man went fishing. The buzzard, the one who steals, swallowed all of the fish and carried them home. The old man lost all of his fish. The buzzard took them all and ran off.

22. *The Bear and Wolf on the Mountain.* (II)

nəmę⁰	*kį·*	*kusəmi⁰*	*hinų'yere*	*saktci'pki·*	*himų're*
Bear	the	corn pounded	who steal	mountain top	who sleep

i'mpi·	*da*	*patkį're.*	*kus*	*katka't⁽here*	*tą'so*	*wá'pkado're.*
fire	the	big [was].	Corn	shelled	wolf [obj.]	feed.

yap patkį'	*wanaku⁰*	*hapatkį're*	*nəmę⁰*	*tugəra're.*	*o'ta*	*pahi'-*
Tree	big	hickory	up big [was]	bear home [was].	He	some

mure	*o'ka*	*wį·rą⁽re*	*kutci'n*	*napkado⁽tci·re.*	*o'ka*	*ni·te'm*
roast	he	eat	bird	his own feed.	He now	all

wi·į'⁽re	*o'ta*	*wi·sərą're*	*we'b⁽hamǫ·'rere*	*tą'si·.*	*o'ta*
[could] eat	him	watch[ed]	[to] catch and eat	wolf.	Him

wi·sara're	*o'ta*	*nəmę'*	*kį.*	*kərį'here*	*we·b⁽hamǫratcu`re*
watch[ed]	him	bear	the.	Good [was]	catch and eat much

wi'dyo	*mą⁽tcuware*	*i·ba'hį·re.*	*du'hri*	*na'dəhere*	*ka*	*we'b⁽hare*
meat	taste sweet	roasted.	Work	hard	the	catch

hi'mba.	*we'b⁽i·re*	*i·ba'tcore.*
sleep[ing].	Caught	roast[ed] much.

The bear who stole some pounded corn on the mountain top was asleep by the big fire. Some shelled corn he fed to the wolf. The bear's home was up in the big hickory tree. For his own feed he roasted and ate some birds. Now, that he had eaten all that he was able to, he watched to catch and eat the wolf. The bear watched him. It was good that he could catch and eat so much meat which tasted sweet when it was roated. He worked hard to catch the wolf sleeping. He caught and roasted him [the wolf].

23. *Tree Frog and Bull Frog Compete in Crying* (III)

kare	*kį'*	*węhatcu're,*	"*do'ka*	*mi·ra⁰suwe,*"
Tree frog	the	was crying hard,	"I now	am better [than you],"

arara'i·   *ki·*   *haduta'tqre.*   *"are'kudyɔre."*   *arara'i̥·*   *ki·*
bull frog   the   so said.   "True now say you."   Bull frog   the

wȩhatcu're.   *tu̥'ki·*   *mu'si·*   *hawa'rɔre*   *ci'rɔci'rɔ*
cried hard.   The little one   got scared   and died   mud all about

hamqtuⁿ   *kawa'rɔre.*   *arara'i̥·*   *ki·*   *haha'hare.*   *ya wa'k^ɛtci·*   *ki'ye*
the in   now died.   Bull frog   the   laughed.   Snake black   the

kuru'k^ɛhɔre.
swallowed him.

FREE TRANSLATION

The tree frog was crying hard. "I am better [at crying than you]," said the bull frog. "How true you speak!" The bull frog cried hard. The little one then got so scared that he died, he died in the mud. Then the bull frog laughed. But the black snake [came along] and swallowed him.

24. *The Boy who was Raised with the Hogs.* (II)

yȩ·tca'wa'   *de^rtcerede'*   *monapani'yere*   *yani*   *ki'*   *motuⁿ*
Child   lost   year one.   Found   the   when

yapsȩta's.   *ntukore're*   *nu'mantu'ndu*   *tci^ɛtci̥^r-*
wood fence made pasture.   Then in come   bell ringing   [imitative

kere   *witkerą'*   *musa'kre*   *musa'derą're*   *nu'mantu'*
exclamation]   hog   with was   with ate   bell ringing

tci̥tci̥^rkere.   *wara'*   *yȩmu'sɔre.*   *itcigneⁿ*   *ukra're*
[imitative exclamation].   Lived   man grown.   Child[ren]   had

nu'manki'   *dukre'bmo'sɔrɔre.*   *witherą'*   *dowa'su'*   *hugnapi'rɔre*
bell the   home kept did.   Hog   bed   down lay

"hisumq   *si*   *tca'kstere*   *nenenaⁿ."*   *hinkawa're.*
"His face hair   feel I   father my."   Somebody [he] thought [it].

"himba^r!   *ha·ha."*   *witkerą'ka*   *ume'*   *tcȩ*
"Yes indeed! [grunting exclamation]."   Hog the now   alone   there

ba'rina.
[he was].

A child was lost for one year. [The child was] found when [they]
made the wood fence in the pasture. Then the hog came in with a
bell tied around its neck ringing ting-a-ling-a-ling. [The child
was accustomed to] eat with the hog with the bell ringing ting-
a-ling-a-ling. The boy lived with the hog until he was a grown man.
The children had taken the bell home and kept it. The boy lay
down in bed with the hog. [He said,] "I feel the hair on my father's
face." He thought it was his father. "Yes, indeed," the pig grunted.
He was alone there with the hog.

25. A Boy Eats a Partridge Raw. (III)

yuksu'naʾ yanəpa' kutcaᵖ kusi yap'tᵊro'   *kida'-*
Mother my   mill   went corn bushel [tree big]   carry on

kora   *bara'naʾ*   *kida'*   *kora.*   *i'kpa*
back going along brother my   carry on back going along. Fence

pida're wədeᵖ tcuᵖithᵊre sᵄ'ya.   *təpəke'kᶜ*   *tu̧təpę̓ wi'pᶜha*
crossed cattle many were scared. Partridge the   small one caught

bara'naʾ   *nᾳpərᾳᵖha*   *hi̧'paʾ*   *mi·.*   *wi·*
brother my   ate completely right away   foot   all but.   All

nᾳpərᾳᵖha.
ate completely right away.

My mother once went to the mill carrying on her back a bushel
of corn, and also carrying [on top of the load of corn] my brother
as she went along. Crossing a fence she met a lot of cattle and was
frightened. [When she put my brother on the ground to enable
her to cross the pasture alone and came back] he had caught a
small partridge and eaten it completely except for a foot.

26. The Child-eating Alligator. (II)

dᵊpᵊhi̧ᵖʾyi̧·   *itci'gᵊni*   *we'bʾoki·re*   *wi·rᾳ'paraᵖ*   *ki·re.*
Terrible alligator   child   catch   eat full.

saptcui're   *yᾳmo̧tuᵖ*   *yapsę̓ᵖtas*   *i·tcuwa're*
Bone[s] much were water in wood fence made (old field)   rest

da'pᾳtcui're.   *patki̧'*   *ki̧·*   *igwa're.*   *tᵊro*   *ki'*   *i·ya'nere*
pond much was.   Big   the   kill[ed].   Big   the   found

dəpəhi·ᵖyi	*tamahi·yu⟨*	*hapri·tcu're*	*do'pa*
terrible alligator	[exclamation of fear]	big much was	something

itcigəni·'	*wi·rą̊tco'*	*patkį'ware*	*nǫ'*	*watcu're.*
child	eats much	big was	fat	very was.

FREE TRANSLATION

An alligator caught a child and ate it completely. Many bones were in the water in the old field and the rest were in the pond. They killed the Big One [the monster]. When they found and killed the big alligator he was big from eating something. He had eaten so many children he was big and very fat.

27. The Flood. (II)

atkani·re'ko	*uksu'tcore*	*i'swą̊'*	*kəraᵖ*	*patkį'hare*	*mo'ną̊*
Long while ago	rain much	river	rise	big [was]	earth

kəpapara'ᵖre	*yę̊'ye*	*iwatərą̊ᵖparą̊ᵖare.*	*a'gre*
under completely [was]	people	washed away completely.	Few

yapha'pi'nare	*są̊'we*	*motuᵖina're*	*utka'ni.*	*tusikį·ye`*	*atkę̊'*
tree up climbed	island	in climb	longtime.	Dove the	far away

ku'tcere	*ko'ratcere.*	*itu'si ki·ye'*	*araske'se*	*ya'pᶜha*	*duho're*
he left	go made.	Dove the	first time for	tree leaf	brought

kat·e'se	*dukha'dukho`re*	*kus*	*doho're*	*dukho'*	*kus*
then time	back came back brought	corn	brought	back	corn

hisumǫᵖ	*duho're.*	*huka't bahi're*	*monɑ'*	*yiraᵖha*	*amaho'tcire.*
his mouth	brought.	Now knew	land	dry	to go to arrive.

uri'rekutəre.
True it is said.

FREE TRANSLATION

A long time ago it rained so much that the river rose and the big earth was completely under the water and the people were washed away. A few climbed up trees on an island [and remained there a] long time. The dove left [and went] far away. The first time the dove came back it brought a leaf back and the next time brought back corn. It brought back corn in its mouth. Now [the people] knew that there was dry land to go to. [This is] true it is said.

WITCHCRAFT.

28. *A Cherokee Witch in the form of an Owl*[1]. (II)

wi·tca'wa dəpę°	yuksoda°	i'ya	nǫ'prəre	yę	mǫtəra'ki·
Night	one	mother my	woman	two	man Cherokee

yębəri'tci·	i·yǫ'kəre	mosa'kəre're.	etusi·ki'ye	i·pi·ki'	wa'
man	woman this	was with.	Owl the	fire the	sitting

pi'k'ha	yapi·hapda're	wat'kat·u'	səwǫ'səwa°kəre.	su'gba
flew	joist upon flew	feathers	stood up all over.	Broom

owətcəka°ha	hagda're	ka°hawa're	nə	mǫtərǫ'	ki·	kusa°hasəta're
using now	took	hit	then	Cherokee the	stopped her

yuha'tare.	uyi'	mǫtərǫ'	ki·	hini·da'ko itare·
prevented. Same as his own	Cherokee	the	he was talking [to owl].

sų'ti·	pi'k'hanǫta're	sakmo sa'həre.	"su'gna-
Out door	flew and left	mountains to whence came.	"House my

maho're	sakoka'	i·ya°wəhəre de'ka i·ya'hrəre mǫ'tərǫ i·ya°.
come in	house now	woman my woman Cherokee woman.

FREE TRANSLATION

One night my mother [was one of] two women who were going home with a Cherokee man. An owl sitting near the fire flew up to a joist [of the house] with its feathers ruffled up all over. The Cherokee making use of a broom hit [the owl] and stopped it from doing anything. In his own language the Cherokee talked [to the owl]. It flew out of the door and left, going to the mountains whence it had come. [Said he] "Into my house, right into my house, here comes that woman, my woman is a Cherokee woman!"

29. *A Cherokee Wrestles with his Wife who is a Witch.* (II)

we'monǫtu're	we'mǫtu°	[mo]nǫtu'	kowa'həre	ki·
Town from coming	town when	in	coming [home]	the

[1] The narrative refers to an incident that took place a number of years ago between George Owl, a Cherokee, who was going with two Catawba women, Margaret Brown and Nancy Harris. He was reputed to have spiritual power and to have communion with witches. Events like these related caused suspicions of his witchcraft in their minds and they both decided not to marry him. To vindicate this opinion of his character, they said he was subsequently shot to death at a feast in the Cherokee Nation.

mǫtu⁰	*wanaku⁰ka*	*i'yakəre'*	*mǫtərǫ́*	*hatəti·'*
when	Hickory [Flat] the	woman this	Cherokee	wrestled with

do'pa	*yętų⁰*	*i·yę́*	*nǫ́'prəre.*	*yuksuna'*	*sǫ-*
something	person small	person	two.	Mother my	was

yatǫ́'re.	*dəpę́*	*tcip'ha*	*iya'kəre*	*yęki'ye*	*mǫtərǫ́'ki·*
frightened.	One	kicked down	woman this	man the	Cherokee

uyi'	*hinda'kǫyα⁰*		*nǫ'həstǫ́'re.*	*"de'ka*
same as himself	spoke to them		left and went home.	"My

i'yanere	*hagwoni'həre."*
woman	follow me."

FREE TRANSLATION

Once when coming from town, having been in town and on the way home at the Hickory Flats this Cherokee woman wrestled with something in the shape of two small persons. My mother was frightened. While she was afraid, this woman kicked down one [of them]. The Cherokee man spoke to them in his own language [and said], "My woman is following me."

30. The Woman who Became an Owl. (II)

yamusi'	*hi·tca'wa*	*i'mpi·*	*ya'ʾmusa*	*terǫ́'rare.*	*ya-*
Woman old	night	fire	road chimney	out went.	Old

musi·'	*ki·*	*nǫ́'prire*	*e'ku*	*bara'yere.*	*ustugri'o'me*
woman	the	two were	these now	sisters were.	Hoot owl alone

ya'katcere	*du'g*	*ya'phapki·wǫ́'re.*	*ustugri'*	*hi·'χhi·'χ*
transformed	home	tree up sat.	Hoot owl	[imitative

	ha'tkire	*yamusi'ki·'ye.*	*dapa ikto'nere*	*ustugri'-*
exclamation]	exclaims	woman old the.	One witch is	hoot owl

kəre	*watkǫ́*	*inu'yere.*
this	chicken	steal.

FREE TRANSLATION

An old woman sitting beside the fire one night went up through the chimney. The two old women were sisters. One had become transformed and had taken the form of a hoot owl and sat up in a tree near her home. The old woman imitated a hoot owl. The one who was a witch took the form of a hoot owl so that she could steal chickens.

31. The Women who Escaped by Transforming Themselves into Animals. (II)

ara'tkanere	*ye*	*imbara'tcure.*	*i̧ya"*	*kawa'are.*
Long time it is	people	not good very.	Woman	some kill.

ya'	*ya'katcere*	*ya'wakatci`*	*ya'katcere*	*ya'kri*	*wapi·re̦"*
Snake	transformed	snake black	transformed	woman this	lizard

ya'katcere	*ya'kri*	*yatciku't'kut*	*ya'katcere.*	*do'po*
transformed	woman this	cricket	transformed.	Something

we^kki·	*i'nere.*	*"ta'yutci·hi'mna?"*	*ume'*	*ha'wi·ru'ire*
cry the	heard.	"Where went to?"	They alone	hide went

ni·te'm	*dug^cro're*	*dugra'yowa".*
all	back again come	again next day.

FREE TRANSLATION

A long time ago some people were not very good. [They were going to] kill some women. One woman became transformed into a blacksnake; another became transformed into a lizard and another into a cricket. Something was heard crying. [They said] "Where did they [the women] go to?" They [the women] all went and hid alone and the next day they came back home again.

32. The Mischievous Dwarfs and How to Avert Them. (II)

ye̦hasu'ri·	*tcuwi'here*	*ya'bwą'muҫrire*	*mo'naka*	*ntugra're.*
People wild	much [are]	in woods live	ground the	in stay.

tcuwi'	*itcigni"*	*we^kkere.*	*hitumǫ'*	*wi'yąre*	*yapte'*	*yapata-*
Much [like]	child	cry.	Acorn	eat	tree root	tree

memi·kәre"	*wi·yą'ki·re*	*kasәmi'"*	*ki·*
around grow	(fungi) eat	turtle stink (mud turtle)	the

watcikәmu"	*ki̧·*	*wi'rąre.*	*ya'pkusa ap*	*itci'gәni·*	*wi·yi'mere^c*
tadpole	the	eat.	Day some	child	carry off.

bo"yąyire	*bo'ki'"*	*yąyire*	*yawa'riwe*	*tą'ntci·*	*baya'rire.*
Shoot you	shot the	you are	you die	cannot	know you [it].

ya	*musi'kərę*	*itci·we'*	*mǫtu"*	*nuwi·"i·re*	*hiską'se*	*nuwi·'*
Woman	old was	pine	to	tie	whose head hair	tie

para"here	*yę suri'ki·ye.*	*[korǫ'bi*	*ya"ore*	*sutki*	*korǫ'bi*
completely	people wild the.	[Colombia	you go	down	Colombia

sak	*krę'tcure].*	*witsagwą'i*	*itu'si*	*i·wą'tcere.*	*di'ską'*
house	pretty much are].	Horse	tail hair	braid.	My head

nəpatciste're	*ndopo'rap*	*ni·tca're.*	*uniat'*	*hwka't'*
I tobacco I rub	then any pain	me cause not.	Then	now

hanere	*deta*	*u'tsere,*	*"du'gare*	*ini·para'ti·na"*	*yęsu'ri.*
here	I	say,	"Again not	me bother come	people wild.

deme'hana`tə	*we"stere*	*yanamusi'sere."*	*namakəri'"hare*
I alone here	cry I	woman I old I am."	Then good are

ini'pare.	*dəpę"*	*inųyere*	*mbara'na'*	*tų'kəre*	*inų'yere*
me bother not.	Once	stole	brother my	little	stole

da'pą'	*du"nare*	*yebhasku"*	*patkį"sakigwa'ntcere.*	*hiksa"*
pond	took	tree stump	big on sat made.	His arm

iwa'sipará"here.	*da'kta*	*ųwati·'rəre·.*	*yęwa"*	*yęhi·ye'tire*
blood suck completely.	Doctor	teach him.	People	water wade

imǫ'tu"	*web"ire*	*web'ki·*	*mǫtu"*	*wa're*	*wi·ye"hare.*
in	catch	catching the	when	die	nearly.

FREE TRANSLATION

Many wild people [dwarfs] live in the woods; they stay in the ground. They cry like children. They eat acorns. Tree roots, and fungi that grows around trees, the stink turtle and tadpoles they eat. Some days they carry off children. If they shoot you, you will die, you cannot know [it]. An old woman was tied to a pine tree by her hair by the wild people. ["Have you been down to Columbia? There are lots of pretty houses in Columbia."] They [dwarfs] will braid a horses tail. I rub tobacco on my head, then they cannot cause me any pain. Then, now I say, "Do not bother me again, wild people. I am alone here, I cry and I am an old woman." They are good, they don't bother me. Once [they] stole my little brother and made him sit on a big tree stump in the pond. [They] sucked the blood out of his arm completely. They taught him to be a doctor. His kin waded in the water to catch him and when they caught him he was nearly dead.

33. Revenge On the Shawnee Raiders. (II)

na'mənəre   sa'waną   itci'gəni   ipkoa're.   yɛyɛ'hinu⁰
Three   Shawnee   child[ren] kill[ed].   People (Catawba) little

ipkoapara⁰re   wi·b'ki're   yɛ'yɛ
kill[ed] completely   [whom they could] catch   people (Catawba)

sa'waną   we'b're.   sa'waną   ki·   we'b'i·gwa're.   hiska⁰-
Shawnee   caught.   Shawnee   the   catch [and] kill.   Whose head

isto're   hiską   yąsuyi'   hapki'pere.   mo'nu-
skin tore off   head   road side   up top [pole] put.   Ground

nituka⁰ere   i·nti·tcui'   sa'ktcipki·.   igiwa're   kora'motu⁰.
in buried   rock much   hill top.   Kill[ed]   came when.

The Shawnee killed three children. All of the little people
[Catawba children] they killed. All of the Catawba people whom
they could catch, the Shawnee caught. The Shawnee were caught
and killed [by the Catawba], their scalps torn off and put up on
a pole by the side of the road. They were buried in the ground on
a hilltop among the rocks. When[ever the Shawnee] came [they
were] killed.

34. A Dog Tells the People how the Tuscarora Killed
his People. (II)

ara't'hanere.   we⁰tcore   tąsi· ki'   yątca⁰   tak
Long while ago it was.   Cry much   dog the   creek   bottom

wawe⁰tcore   dome'dugrei'ru'i·ba'ri.
cry much   those alone at home [someone] were come [and] kill.

yɛ   paį⁰hare.   yɛtcui'   kɛ'sa   i'rure   yɛ-
People none were.   People much   [from] far off   come   people

imbara   i·rio're   yɛ   ta'skara'.   uniat' tąsi· ki· yinterowa⁰
not good   come   people Tuscarora.   Then   dog the   child

tu'ŋki   tasi' ka'   takəre're.   ta'si· tu'ŋki   kusta⁰   du'raku'nere.
little   dog the now   by stay.   Dog little   corn bread   brought.

mu'sirere'ʻ   yintəra'ki·   hi'ŋkui·re   sakmotu⁰   a'tkanihat'
Grew up   child the   who stay   mountain on   long while

ku' tcere	*mṵsi'tcere.*	*tą̄si·*	*ki̥·*	*we̜⁽tcore*	*su' kpa꜔mǫtu꜔ra' re*
it is told	raised him.	Dog	the	cry much	house some in go

we̜⁽tcore	"tani	*ku' dyǝne꜔ ?*"		"ye	*ni·te'm*	*i·wa' re.*"
cry much,	"What	now you [ails] ?"		"People	all	killed."

	"taį̌ tciba' yane꜔ ?"	"mbarese' rere	da' ni·re!"		*sa' kmǫtu꜔*
	"How do know you ?"	"Know I do	I saw [it]!"		Mountain on

ya' ni·re."	*yudu' grore.*
you [will] see [him]."	Home went [and brought].

It was a long time ago. A dog was crying by the bottom of the creek, crying much. Those who were alone at home someone had come and killed. There were no people. Many people from far off had come — the people who are not good, the Tuscarora, had come. Then the dog stayed by the little child. The dog brought [him] corn bread. The child grew up on the mountain side where they stayed a long time and [the dog] raised him, it is told. The dog went into a house and cried, cried. "What ails you now?" they asked. "My people are all killed," he answered. "How do you know?" they said. He said, "I do know. I saw it. Go on the mountain and you will see him." They went and took him [the boy] home.

35. *The Catawba Kill a Chickasaw and Put him inside his Horse's Belly.* (III)

i·ye'wi	*mąterą꜔tcut·e'hǝre.*	*kwɔ'*	*parą꜔hǝre*	*yɛa'wi.*
People	land outside different.	Kill	away	people many.

kwɔ·	*parą꜔hǝre*	*tcirikhatcę꜔*	*akę́ hotcu'we.*	*yę*	*imbara' hǝre.*
Kill	away	run away	far very.	People	mean.

arat⁽ka'nǝre	*i·ye' yętcu'wi*	*ita' na꜔.*	*yę*	*tcikǝsa'*	*dǝpę́*
Long ago long	people many	said.	Man	Chickasaw	one

hę꜔	*i·ya'*	*nąprere'*	*iru' re.*	*i·yę́ mǫtce' hǝre*[1]	*yębǝri'tcę꜔*	*hę꜔*
the	woman	two	come.	People wild	man	the

ya'	*ną́ pǝri·꜔*	*ko̜⁽hrere.*	*yę*	*kru' gi·hǝre*	*nite'mp⁽*	*yą́ sahrere.*
woman	two	with.	People	drinking	all	drunk.

---

[1] *i·mǫ́ tce* means "sing" as well as "wild, savage", so the term denoting the Chickasaw Indians may mean "Singing People" as well as "Savage People".

yi'yę' kį· i·gwa'hɘre wi·tsɘgwą'i· i·gwa're pɔ·se'hɘre yę'
People the kill [him] horse kill belly cut open man

he" pɔ·tuke'hɘre. hi·ską" itusa" tuksa'pɘre mǫtuke'hɘre.
the belly in put. His head tail in stick ground in buried.

FREE TRANSLATION

The people [who lived on the] land outside [were] different. [They] killed off many people. [They] killed off [the people and] ran away, far, far away. [They were] mean people. Long, long ago [there were] many people [it was] said. One Chickasaw man and two women came. [They were] wild people, the man [and] the two women together. The people were all drinking [and] all [got] drunk. The people killed him and killed his horse. They cut the horse's belly open and put the man in its belly. His head they stuck toward the tail and buried him in the ground.

36. *The Woman, the Deer and the Wolf.* (II)

ara'dre⟨ dɘpɘna'tki·re sakhabra'
Long time ago one [who] hunts (hunter) mountain on somewhere

wi·dɘbo'ye na'pri· kawa're. nɘpę' du'gdugra're yamusi' ki·
deer two kill. One home bring woman old the,

"di·ra'hode." yamusi' ki· daduho're wi·ya' ki't'here
"Go bring." Woman old the went to get [it] cord break,

"wi·yaa' kit'kit'opo' ⟨hatki're." *wi·dɘbo'ye huktuki'tcere*
"Cord break off [exclamation]." Deer down drop caused

kau̯'hatcure yamusi'ki·ye·. ya'kį· ya'tci· hį'pa'
cry much woman old the. Woman the ashes who foot

hata'tukere, "hani·do" nkatsɘną'". ye'ki·ye yentca" ki·
in from fell, "What then now I ?" Man the (Shawnee) boy the

ra"here dutci'rik'hare odopo' dutciri'k'hare wi·dyoki' i·ba'rire.
and with take run thing take run deer meat the roast.

Sawaną" pi'k'i·re. "naci·ani'tcere" "wiri'k'hade na-
Shawnee fly up. "I am afraid made." "Don't say it! I am

ciatco're sawaną' imba'ri atcu're!" yamusi'ki· ho're
afraid much Shawnee bad very!" Woman old the come,

"do're sukɘrį·"tcure. do're yamusa'ne' ?" "nde't' bara're."
"What smell nice so. What in fire ?" "I know not."

pa'ksutcore.	*"ye'ta'*	*ya'dopoyane' ?"*	*"saktci'pkira*
Lied much.	"You	you thing get where?"	"Mountain top and

kawa're	*sa'ktcipki·ra*	*tciri'khatcu'hukore*	*yapkose'*
go on	mountain top and	run much go	tree against

patcikaᵖsere.	*ha'koare*	*handa't'* *ka't'here.*	*tusəpᵩseᵖ*
bump it.	Down die	who neck break.	Pot legged (cooking pot)

ntukai'here	*ha'rotcutcu`re."*	*tasi su'ri ki·'* *e'rore*	*"i'yet*
then in put	boil make much."	Dog wild the come	"People

yi·paᵖharayane' ?"	*"wa'hari!"*	*i'gwanta're*	*mitce'hi'ware.*
people foot [step] see you?"	"No!"	Kill [her] we	dont say.

tᵩ'si·suri'	*i·swᵩᵖ*	*mᵩterᵩᵖ*	*yapki'*	*yapha'pərare*
Dog wild	river	out in	tree the	tree up went (climb)

hinda' kiye	*yamuri're.*	*i'swᵩ'* *mᵩtuᵖrere*	*yapha'*
who shadow the	in water was.	River in went	tree leaf

hisumᵩᵖ	*pᵩ'here.*
who mouth	full.

FREE TRANSLATION

A long time ago a hunter somewhere out on the mountain killed two deer. He took one home [and told] the old woman, "Go bring [the other]." The old woman went to get [it]. [And the] cord with which she tied it broke. "[The] cord broke off", she exclaimed. The deer dropped down and the old woman cried. The old woman fell and burned her foot in the ashes. "Now what am I going to do?" [She said]. The man [Shawnee] and the boy [Shawnee] the thing took and ran off with it and roasted the deer meat. [When the] Shawnee [appeared] she said, "I am frightened." [Don't say that you are so very much afraid of the Shawnee. They are very bad.] The old woman came and said, "What smells so nice? What is in the fire?" "I do not know," the man said. He lied. "Where did you get that thing?" They said, "We went on the mountain top and on the mountain top we made it run and bump against a tree. It broke its neck and fell down dead. We then put it in a cooking pot and boiled it. The wolf came and the people said, "Did you see the footprints of any people?" "No", he said. "Don't say [we] killed her".

(The[1] wolf went out in the river [after] the one who climbed up the tree (the opossum) and whose shadow was in the water. [The wolf] went in the river [and got his] mouth full of tree leaves.

---

[1] This section does not belong in the story but is a part of text 16.

PART II
FOLK BELIEFS

REPTILES.

37. Legend of the Ancient Indian Town and the Monster Water Serpent. (II)

sukətəba⁗	*sębę' hǝre*	*ara' tį̇*	*yętcu wi'tare*	*i'bare*
Town	ancient was	long ago	people many were	dancing

tcu' ki·	*ta'nǫ.*	*ha'naha*	*wǝha⁗hare*	*i·wa're*	*parą⁗hę*	*hį̇'we*
much the.		All	disappeared	died away did		may be

apǝte'	*hį̇·*	*hahį̇'re.*	*iswą⁗təri*	*po⁗ta're*	*yętca'*	*dǝpę'*	*de'tc⁗tare.*
few	the	we left.	River across	wade	a boy	one	lost.

ya'	*wi'pare*	*ya'kį̇·*	*wi'p⁗hare.*	*ya'kį̇·*
Snake	caught him	snake the	caught him.	Snake the

wi'bi·tare	*igwa'tare*	*i·ti· patkį̇' ki·*	*yębri·tci*
they caught him.	Killed him [on]	stone big the	men

kre'bǝma	*igwa're.*	*ya'kį̇·*	*yętca'*	*dǝtau*	*kamo'tǝre*	*it⁗ma*
caught	killed.	Snake the	boy	his neck	sucked	blood

kamo'tǝre.
sucked.

FREE TRANSLATION

The "ancient; everlasting" town was long ago (the home of) many people — much dancing there. All have now disappeared; died off it seems except the few of us who are left. Once a boy waded across the river there and was lost. A snake caught him. And they caught the snake and killed it on a big stone. It was the men who caught and killed it. The snake had sucked the boy's neck; had sucked out the blood[1].

---

[1] A similar tale is found recorded in 1737 among the Indians of North Carolina, by John Brickell (The Natural History of North Carolina. Dublin, 1737, p. 371). It tells of a monster snake that killed many Indians until finally it was destroyed by an eagle.

38. Monster Water Snake Crushes Children. (III)

ya	hąmo⁰	ya	i·swą'	yę	tca'
Snake	in water	snake	monster (chief)	person	branch (child)

we'b'hɘre	dugɘre'	hana'we.	ya'	kį·	yętca'	kį·	akwa're.
catch	back again	never.	Snake	the	child	the	kill.

ya'	kį·	yę'tca	kį·	nowę'hɘre.	ya	hamǫ'wąkį·ye.
Snake	the	child	the	envelop.	Snake	in water lying the.

FREE TRANSLATION

A monster water snake caught a child [and it] never [came] back again. The snake killed the child. The snake was lying in the water and it enveloped the child.

39. The Monster Leech. (III)

wɘtc'kɘmǫ⁰	do'pɘ	tca	ha're	į'ti·	kį·	kɘpa'	parą⁰hɘre.
Leech	thing	so	large	rock	the	covered	entirely.

FREE TRANSLATION

A leech, a thing so large it was, that it covered a rock completely.

(This hideous creature lived in the river and was occasionally seen by the Indians spread over a large boulder. It is still believed to exist somewhere down the river.)

40. The Glass Snake. (III)

ya	kat'ka'tɘre	ka⁰mǫtu⁰	ka't
Snake	breaks in pieces [Glass Snake]	hit when	breaks

katɘparą⁰ha	kat'to'tɘpɘre.	paha'wɘkeha⁰
in pieces entirely	breaks up.	Somewhere hides itself [says],

"tca'hawɘtca'we."	i'tkutnaparą'	howe
"I will cause myself to hide."	Joins itself together	completely can

tɘpę'.	yamuke'	ha	waha'we	itkutna'we.
into one.	Put it in fire	now	if not	join together will.

4*

The Glass Snake breaks in pieces, when hit it breaks entirely
to pieces. It hides itself somewhere, saying, "I will cause myself
to hide." It can join itself completely together into one. But if
put in the fire, it will not join together again.

41. The Whip-Snake. (III)

ya	yi·ha'hawa	nowe'ya'ya'hi·we	web'ya	yiha"owe
Snake	whip	tie may you may	catch you	he may whip you

dowe"kwi·nawe.
will be no good any more.

The whip snake may tie you [envelop you] catch you and whip
you, after which you will be no good.

42. The Salamander Barking — a Death Omen. (III)

ta'si·	tuhi·nu̧'	monatu'grare[1]	wo"hɘre	yawa'ri·we.
Dog	little tiny	ground down in	barks at you	you die will.

If the tiny-ground-dog barks at you, you will die.

BIRDS.

43. The Wren Causes Laziness. Do not Touch its Nest. (III)

kutci'n	tɘro"tɘro"	tɘpɘ'e'tcu're	dowɔ's	monoka'tcɘre.
Bird	small very [wren]	lazy very	nest	on ground makes.

mo̧tca'gi·tce"	a'na	tɘpɘ'e'atcu'we.	kɘri̧	haha'we
In hand put	do not lest	lazy we may be.	Good	not at all will be

kɘri̧'habara'we.
good luck not we will have.

The small bird [a wren][2] is very lazy. It makes its nest on the
ground. Do not put your hand on it lest you may become lazy. That
will not be good, we shall not have good luck.

[1] The phrase denotes salamanders in general.
[2] The house wren (Troglodytes aedon) was indicated though it would seem
to be an error.

44. *The Wren is Lazy.* (III)

kutci'n   tṵtǝro'   tǝp'e'hǝre   tcṵ'wi·   pǝkǫ°nahi·we.
Bird   small, small   lazy   is worms   he gets to eat.

FREE TRANSLATION

The tiny lazy bird (house wren) searches for and gets worms.

45. *Bird Calls a Sign of Someone Coming.* (I)

yę'pa   ha'wǝhę°   sṵ'ti·homǫtu°   kutci'n wehahę°.   Kutcin
Somebody   coming   door around when   birds   calling.   Birds

ni·da'ehę°.
talking.

FREE TRANSLATION

Some body is coming when around the door birds are calling. The birds are talking.

46. *The Whippoorwill's Hat is the Lady Slipper.* (III)

wit kuyǫ'[1]   hiska'so   ki·[2]   mǫ sapᶜhowe   yararǫ'   mǫtu
Whippoorwill   his hat   the   on head puts   spring   when

węᶜtcuwe.
he cries forth.

FREE TRANSLATION

The whippoorwill puts his hat on his head when spring comes, and cries forth.

47. *The Humming Bird was Made from Man's Breath.* (III)

kutcę sǝri'sǝri·hǝre[3]   yęye'katcǝre   yę   bri'tci.   wa't tu
Bird   sucking   man made him   Indian man.   Dandelion-down

hi'ksumu°   bo'kᶜhapuᶜhǝre.   mǫ +   pi'kᶜhǝre.   yę'   pi'ktcǝre.
his hand   put in   blew.   Yes!   He flew off.   Man   very smart.

---

[1] Name derived from call of the bird (Antrostomus vociferus).

[2] The native designation for the pink lady slipper (Cypripedium acaule). It is worth noting that while everywhere imaginative ideas are associated with it, no recorded information from other eastern tribes gives a notion corresponding to the above. The Catawba hold the belief that the bird is never heard to call until the lady slipper is in bloom, that he waits for it to open so that he can wear it as a hat.

[3] Ruby-Throated Humming Bird (Archilochus colubris).

The humming (sucking) bird was created by man, an Indian man. He took — plant down in his hand and blew upon it and, verily — the bird flew off. He was a smart man.

48. *Seeing the Cardinal is a Sign of an Unexpected Occurrence.* (III).

kutci'n	*səke^{o1}*	*pi'kəhqwəre*	*hị'pa*	*hawe*	*hị·'we,*	*do'pa*
Bird	red	flying up	something	coming	probably,	something

nitcị·ka^p	*awa'həre.*
sudden now	not expected [possibly a death].

The red bird flying up is a sign of someone coming, of something unexpected suddenly happening.

49. *The Errant Blue Jay.* (III)

ti·nde'	*ki·*	*kore*	*yɑp*	*na'mənere*	*ka*	*duk^{c}ho'we.*
Blue-jay	the	gone	days	three	now	back will come.

yẹmbara'		*buk^{c}u'tcere*	*ya'wutẹ'*	*duk^{c}ho'rəre.*
Man bad [Evil spirit]		goes down to	sand	takes with him.

The Blue-jay[2] goes away [on Saturday] in three days comes back [Tuesday]. He goes to [see the Bad Man] and takes sand with him.

50. *Owls Crying are Omens of Good News.* (III)

iswɑ^p	*hi·tak*	*atuse'*	*ta*	*wewe^{y}kire.*	*wi·mba'həre*	*we^{y}i*	*ki·*
River	across	dove	the	cries.	Over-river owl	crying	the

tare.	*istu'gri·*	*we·^{c}kire,*	*wi·mba'ta*	*we^{k}kire,*
makes.	Great horned owl	cries,	Over-river owl	cries,

wi'yu	*kərẹ^{y}ha*	*ha'niwe*	*sugəki'ro*	*we^{y}kire.*
news	good	hear will	close to house and	cries.

---

[1] Cardinal (Cardinalis cardinalis).

[2] Cyanocitta cristata.

Across the river the mourning dove[1] cries. The over-river owl[2] makes the crying, then the great horned owl[3] cries, and the over-river owl cries again, "Good, news may soon be heard, close to the house," he cries.

CHARMS.

51. Nature Rejoicing after a Snow Storm — A Weather Charm. (III)

wi·tca′ware	*tcį·′tcure*	*wa'watcu′re*	*kutci′n*	*yuwi·ǫsi·''hǝre.*
Last night	cold very	snow much	birds	were hungry.

yawi′kha'	*nų′ti*	*į′ti·sa′mǫtu*	*ha′p'tci·wikha''*	*ya*	*wik'ha'*
Warm	sun	on rock comes out	shining hot	hot	the now

kǝrį·tcu′re.	*kutci′n*	*kį·*	*imuse′rǝre.*	*kutci′n*	*ki*	*we''*	*ki·*	*tcapana''*
nice very.	Birds	the	are glad.	Birds	the	crying		somewhere

imamǫ′rǝre.	*yapǝtę́*	*pa*	*sǝwǫku′we*	*kutci′n*	*pa'*
roost.	Board flat [trap]	some	we set will	bird	some

hagwa′harǫ′we.	*yap isi′gǝrǝre*	*ya′tci·*	*buka′we*	*mǫtu''*
kill and eat we may.	Day bad	ashes	throw out may	when

ayǫkǝrį''howe.	*ǝtus*	*ta''we*	*tcuwi'atcuwe*	*ǝtus*	*igda′we*
clear off nice may.	Pots	make will	lots make will	pots	go trade

tcapana′.	*do′pa*	*hari·harǫ′we.*	*hatana′ka*	*do′pa*
somewhere.	Something	hunt to eat will.	Now	something

ha′ne' ?	*harǫ′we*	*do′pa*	*du′ri·a′he*	*nawe.*
is there ?	We eat	something	to work at	let us.

Last night was very cold, much snow. The birds were hungry. The sun comes out now warm and shining hotly so now it is hot and very nice. The birds are glad. The birds are crying somewhere from their roost. We will set some fall-traps to kill some birds to eat. On a bad day throw out ashes, it may clear off nice. Then we can make pots, lots of pots, and go trade them somewhere to hunt something to eat. Now will we eat something? Let us get some work.

---

[1] Zenaidura macroura carolinensis.

[2] Local name for the Barred Owl (Strix varia).

[3] Bubo virginianus.

52. A Prayer-Charm for Good Weather. (II)

ya'tci	ba'k'here	tci'ʔǫntcore	wę'ya	hawoᶜnaire.
Ashes	thrown out	cold much	windy	thanks say.

yawi'k	itina'	yawi'k	si·ʼ	usi'	kitina'.
[tomorrow] warm	come	[tomorrow] warm	nice	weather	come.

FREE TRANSLATION

When it is cold and windy, throw out ashes and say, "Thanks." Tomorrow it will become warmer. Tomorrow nice warm weather will come.

53. The Rabbit's Foot as a Love Charm. (I)

dəpəhwą'	hį·pa'ʔ	ǫwətcəhę'ʔ	yępa'ʔ	imosa'tcəhę'.	hį·pa'ʔ
Rabbit	his foot	using	person some	love cause.	His foot

ǫwətcəʔ	bakəta'wǫtcəhę'.	uniatᶜ	imosa'hę'.
using	neck use it.	Then	he love.

FREE TRANSLATION

Rabbit foot using will make anyone love another. Use the foot around [the person's] neck. Then he [or she] will love.

54. Red-blossom for Luck Charm. (III)

sęwə	səke'ʔ	ka	su'k·usua'we	duruk·į·-
Blossom	red	the now	house (?) (keep) we	good luck the

tcu'we.	sənu'mi·	ha'ni·we	sənu'səkę'	sənu'təpį·sa'
much be.	Money some	get may	money red (gold)	money paper

tcuwi're.	mi·	ha'ne	hanu.
much.	Some	get	may.

FREE TRANSLATION

We keep a red blossom[1] in the house now to bring much good luck. We may get some money — gold money, much paper money. We may get some.

OMENS.

55. The Ground Hog and his Shadow. (III)

monoą'	tu'gərą'	wi·yi·hį'nda	ka'niwe	sąya	nǫ'tuwe.
Ground	in hog	own his shadow	sees if	scared	go back may.

---

[1] Unidentified botanically.

oyi·hį́nda	*ka'niwe*	*mo'na*	*tuk*	*utcɔre*	*yap'ɔsi'-*
His own shadow	sees	ground	in	back goes	days weather

gri·re.
spoiled be.

If the ground hog sees his own shadow he is scared and will go back. If he sees his own shadow he goes back in the ground and the weather will be bad.

56. *The Omen of the Falling Star.* (II)

wapi'tnu	*soͨ͞tcui're*	*dopa*	*tcui'ta*	*bahą́ hire.*	*hapaki*
Star	fall much	some	trouble	some not know.	up bright

dop'a	*tcui'hį·*	*bahą́'re*	*wapi'tnu*	*soͨ͞tcui·re*	*yę*	*sębe'*
some	trouble.	Who knew	star	fall much	people	ancient

aica'tcure	*ta'ntca*	*hamba`re.*
fear much	could	not sleep.

[A] falling star [means unforseen] trouble. [When it shows] up bright [it means] some trouble [is coming.] The ancient people, [when they] knew [that a] star had fallen [they were so frightened that they] could not sleep.

57. *Snow Birds a Sign of Snow or Sleet.* (III)

sɔnu'	*sure'*		*tcuwi're*	*wa'wo'we*	*u'ktcowe.*
Money	wild	(money bird)	many	snow may	sleet (rain) may.

When many wild money [birds are seen] snow or sleet may [be expected].

58. *Crows Cawing Means Clear Weather.* (III)

e'	*we'tci·*	*mǫtu't͆*	*ąyą́'we.*	*e'*	*kį·*	*we'tcu*
Crow	crying	when	clear will be.	Crow	the	cry much

mǫtu"hɔre	*i·swą́'hiak*	*i·swą́'tak*	*wik͆kɔrę́*	*tcuwe.*
when does	river across	[river down]	warm nice	very will.

When the crow cries it will be clear. When the crow is crying much, down and across the river, it will be nice and warm.

59. *When Red Root Blossoms, Terrapin Lays its Eggs.* (III)

kaya'	kį	pa'ro	mǫtu"	ta'ktu	sį'wə	mǫtu"
Terrapin	the	comes out	when	red root	blooms	when

i·nu'wuwe.
laying [eggs] will.

The terrapin comes out when the red root blossoms, and will lay its eggs.

60. *Sign of Burning Soot in the Chimney.* (II).

itisi'	į·pi'	wi·rą'	wi·dyo'	ya'ndəre	bi·hará're	hi'we.
Soot	fire	burn	meat	fresh	we eat	will.

[When] soot burns [in the] fire [chimney] [we will have] fresh meat [to] eat.

61. *Dreams of Luck.* (III)

"dowe'	yamusi'gri	ne	hitca'wa?	yamusi'gri	kərį'yəne'?"
"What	your dream		last night?	Your dream	good you did?"

witca'wa	ya"	dəsəbatcu're	na'musigri	mbara're.	witca'wa
Night	snake	bothers much	my dream	bad.	Night

namusi'gri	sənu'	tcuwi'həre	dəru'kʻhatcu're.	witca'wase'	na'musigri
my dream	money	much	luck very.	Night this	my dream

paį'ha're	na'musi'gri	ni'hare.
nothing,	my dream	not a bit.

"What did you dream last night? Your dream, was it good?" [At night if] snakes bother me, my dream is bad. At night, if I dream of much money, [that is] very [good] luck. Last night I dreamed of nothing, I dreamed not a bit.

62. *How to Avert Bad Luck when Meeting a Woman while Hunting.* (III)

yę	dapayaⁿəne?		ya'	ki·	etapaⁿhowe	mbara'tą're.
Man	going hunting is it ?		Woman	the	meets will	bad was.

dowe'	igwa'we	ya'	ki· itapaⁿ	ki·ye	yą	təro'həre.	yą	ki'
Nothing	kill will	woman	the meet	the	road	big.	Road	the

hagrade	kəsą'hade	wutcu'hade	mątci'hade	kəri·howe.
cross on do	mark make	spit do	spit on it	all right will be.

FREE TRANSLATION

So is the man going hunting ? Should he meet a woman it would be bad luck. He would kill nothing if he meets the woman on a big road. [Make] a cross on the road, mark it, spit, spit on it and it will be good [luck].

63. *Sticks Turn into Snakes to Guard a Melon Patch.* (III)

yę	musi'	yap	hi·tce'rəre	muka'həre	sə'rəbǫ'ri·	monakəri'həre.
Man	old	stick	sharp	ground put	melon patch	land good.

yę'pa	sərəb	i·nų'rəre.	ya	tcuwi'həre	yapəre'	musa'wa
Person	some	melon steal.	Snake	many	stick	come from

tcuwi'həre	ya.	yę	tciri'k^ʿhəre.
many	snake.	Person	run away.

FREE TRANSLATION

An old man stuck sharp sticks in the ground in his melon patch. The land was good. Some person stole some melons. Many snakes came from the sticks. The person ran away.

MISCELLANEOUS BELIEFS.

64. *Thrust Iron into Fire to Drive away Witch-Owl.* (III)

hǫ hǫ	we^ʿhəre	ka'ų	hatcu're,	dəro'b	yamu	keⁿa'we	i'pi
Barred-owl	cry	wail	much,	iron	in fire	put we	fire

muke'hade	hǫhǫ'	ki·	wi'k^ʿhowe.
in put do	barred-owl	the	quiet may.

When the barred-owl cries and wails we put an iron in the
fire so that the barred-owl will keep quiet.

65. Belief Concerning Crawfish in Springs. (II)

i'sę   *wi·harą́re kurį́here.*   *yęsebe'*   *i·ra'tąre yąntce·i'-*
Crawfish   fried   good are. People ancient believe   spring

ni·te'm   *hapa'bakare*   *i'sę*   *kį'*   *yi·raᵖaure.*
all   throw [them] out on bank   crawfish   the   dry go.

Crawfish are good fried. The ancient people believed that if
the crawfish were thrown out of the spring onto the bank, the spring
would go dry.

66. How Storms Arise in the Mountains. (III)

ye'hotcu're   *sakmǫtuᵛ*   *sa'hǝre*   *waʾwatcu'hǝre*   *sakmǫ-*
Wind in strong   mountains in   comes out   snow much   mountains

sa'wǝre   *mǫhiᵛ*   *tcuwį're.*   *ya'pǝ si'grǝri·tcu're.*
comes from   ice   lots of it.   Day   bad very.

Strong winds come from among the mountains, quantities of
snow come from among the mountains and lots of ice — that's
very bad weather.

67. Ghosts. (III)

wi·tca'use   *wi·tcau dara'ha*   *ene'mǫtuᵛ*   *ye' wi·*
Tonight   night middle [mid-night]   heard when   people the

koto'newe   *mo'wǝʾe'weʾ*   *mǫkᶜtci·mǫ'hade*   *kǝrįᵛhade.*
ghosts the   wandering about will be   pray do   be good.

yę   *imbara'*   *imaᶜrǝre.*   *yę*   *sębe'he*   *itcigni'*
Persons   bad   dont sleep.   People   ancient the   children

yę   *tca'tcǝre.*   *tciri'k*   *ha'tcǝde.*   *sayaᶜtcǝde.*
persons   who frighten.   Run away   make them.   Scare them.

Tonight at midnight when the ghosts will be heard wandering about, you must pray to be good. Bad people do not sleep [then]. The ancient people are those who frighten children. Make them run away! Scare them off!

PRAYERS.

68. Prayer to Avert a Thunder Storm. (II)

ara'tkanǝre	*yęyę*	*sębe're*	*moyo't'kamo"kire*	*yehotcui'-*
Long while ago	people	ancient	pray[ed] sing	storm much

hǫre.	*uksotcui'*	*ha'aure.*	*hatat'hi'wǝre*	*ni·te'm*
coming (cyclone).	Rain much	come.	In front	all

sǝwa'ŋk'hitsa	*maho'tka*	*mǫ'hi're*	*ume*	*iksa'*	*hapǫ'rǝre*
stand up	pray	sing	alone	hand	outspread

"wa'ri·we	*hakpi*	*nų'ntcide*	*hi·yę'*	*ki·.*	*nita'wohu're*
"Never dies (God)	up	help us	who people	the.	Divide

hotcui·	*haure*	*ki'*	*hawo"naitcu're*	*ninta'mohakpina'."*
storm much	come	the	thank say much	us protect [and] help."

A long while ago, the ancient people would pray and sing when a bad storm was coming, when it was going to rain much. They would all stand up in front and pray and sing with hands outspread. "God above, help us, the people. Divide the storm so that it will not come, we say thanks, protect and help us."

69. Prayer to Avert a Cyclonic Storm. (III)

yetcuwi'	*haure.*	*yeki·*	*ki'kato'*	*parǫ"hure*	*mǫktci*
Wind much	come.	Wind the	scatter	roll away	pray

mahade.	*wa'riwe*	*hak'pi·nųtc·we*	*hawo"*
do.	Never dies (God)	over watch may	(exclamation) thanks!

Much wind is coming. Scatter the wind and roll away [the cloud], pray do. May God watch over us: Thanks!

70. Prayer for Night's Rest. (III)

hokəpi'	*wi·tca'wəse.*	*ya'uhi'ak*	*depę̌'.*	*hokəpi'*
Lie down	night this.	Daylight through	one.	Lie down

haːci·wa'we	*ya'uhi·ak*	*kəre'*	*dəpę̌'ha'ni·we.*
rest we	daylight through	good	[another] one see may.

FREE TRANSLATION

We lie down this night. Another day we have lived through.
We lie down to rest [hoping that through your] good[ness] we
may see through the daylight of another day.

71. Supplication (III)

kərə^ʔ	*a'we*	*waha'*	*mǫtu'*	*yę̌'*	*mbara'*	*kəpe*
Good	we	not	when	person	bad	lies [the Devil]

mǫ'na'we.	*kərę̌'a'we*	*si·mba're*	*mǫ'na'we.*
go we may.	Good we	Heaven	go we may.

FREE TRANSLATION

When we [are] not good, when persons are bad [and] tell lies,
we may go [with] the Devil. If we are good we may go to Heaven.

TABOOS.

72. Against Going into a Corn-Crib for Three Days after a Death. (I)

yępawa'rit'	*ku's*	*suk*	*su'nti*	*ka'rak*	*wa'hę̌ʔ*	*yab*
Person any dying	corn	house	door	open	not	day

na'mənehę̌ʔ.	*ya'tci·*	*baguap'*	*yab*	*na'mənehę̌'*,	*yę̌*	*wa'ri*
three.	Ashes	throw	not	day three,	person	dead

kị·ye	*akotuke'wap'*	*yab*	*na'mənehę̌'.*
the	talk about do not	day	three.

FREE TRANSLATION

When a person dies the corn-crib door is not opened for three
days, and the deceased is not mentioned for three days[1].

---

[1] This taboo probably indicates that the soul of the deceased was believed
to remain about the scenes of life for three days. It seems that the Cherokee
hold a similar belief, since they do not enter the corn-crib for any purpose
for the same length of time, fearing that the "corn will all disappear if they
do". I was told, however, that the Cherokee do not have the ruling about
throwing out the ashes of the fire.

73. Against Burning Sassafras Wood. (I)

ku'stapi'	*ǫwǝtca"*	*ųyawa'he'*	*įpi'*	*mǫtu"*	*ya'ra*	*mǫtu*
Sassafras	using	burn not	fire	in	summer	in

yapakso"tce'.
you tell lie dont.

Do not burn sassafras wood in the summer, or you will tell lies.

The taboo against burning sassafras, and grape-vine as well, is quite widely observed among the southeastern tribes, as far north as the Powhatan peoples of Virginia all of whom, even today, are faithful to the belief.

74. Against Making Fire and Smoke before the Moon. (III)

kǝrį·	*yaha're*	*ya'pse*	*nųnti'*	*ani·*	*kǝpi'*	*mǫtu"*	*ya'pitę̨'*
Good not	is	Sunday	moon	build	fire	when	cut wood [brush]

wirą'tcǝre	*į'pi*	*da'tcu*	*suksu"tcure*	*nųnti'*	*i'ndǝre.*
burn make	fire	make	smoke much	moon	new.

It is not good, [especially when it is] Sunday, to build fire [under the moon[1]] or to set fire to brush, or make a fire [to cause] much smoke, especially when the moon is new.

75. Taboo for Widows. (I)

ya ya'mpi·	*ta'ntci*	*yępa"*	*kura'hę"*	*monoda'panihę".*
Widow	can not	person any	speak	year one.

A widow must not speak to anyone for a year, [outside of her own family].

76. Against Cooking Deer and Turkey Meat Together. (II)

wi·dǝboyo"	*hi·'*	*watkątǝro'yo*	*hį·'*	*ni·te'mphi'ri*	*ną'prip*
Deer meat	the	and turkey meat	the	all	both

---

[1] The Catawba consider the moon to be male the sun female.

hakba´kәre itus   motu"   kurį"hahare.
mix in   pot   in   good not.

FREE TRANSLATION

It is not good to mix both the deer meat and the turkey meat in one pot.

SONGS.

77a. Song Used when Washing Children in the Creek. (II)

yu[1] mi tą' na tu ha tcin tu

pra ne waŋk ya wakas dat kose

tu   kųm ⟨
in   plunge.

77b. Verse for Blind Man's March Game. (II)

to" tahan to", to" tahan to"[2].
Where am I going?

---

[1] The syllables have the sense of counting out. Mrs. Brown suggested only disconnected meanings, *ya = woman, dat kose = deep hole.*

[2] The translation is not exact.

PART III.

MEDICINE PRACTICES.

78. *Ghosts the Cause of Disease.* (III)

yɛhį·da'	*yɛwakəto'ne*	*wi·tca'wa*	*atu's kį·*[1]	*nǫ'prəre*	*yɛ*
Person shadow	person ghost	at night	o'clock	two	man

musi·'	*ki·*	*duk'ho'we*	*nǫwaresatcu're.*	*ntu*	*wa'riwe*	*nasa're-*
old	that	back come	I be sick very.	Then	die may	I sorry

tcu'we.	*ya'brare*	*du'wehǫca'rəre*	*wį·ti·*	*ki'*	*hakatca"*
very may.	Daylight come	I will not fear	medicine	the	use make

kəruk'hu'we	*kərį'huwe*	*mi'barehu'we.*
drink will	do good will	get better will.

FREE TRANSLATION

[When] the shade, or shadow, of a dead person — a ghost — comes at two o'clock in the night; that old man coming back — I will become very sick. And I may even die. I should be very sorry. [But when] daylight comes I will no longer be afraid, but will make and use medicine and will drink it which will do me good and I shall become well.

79. *Sickness Caused by Eating Pipe Clay.* (III)

atu's	*ta'a*	*mǫtu"*	*į·tu"*	*kį·*	*mi·harǫ'we.*	*wi·į're*
Pot	make	when	clay	the	eat some will.	It is eaten

yapǫ"i·we.	*asəwə'harǫwe*	*į'tu'*	*kəri·ha're*
wormy will be.	A quantity eat we will	clay	good not is

wa'resatcu're	*sabme'hiwe*	*yį·təro'ki'kəre'*
sick very	poor like will be (lit. "bone only")	child born

---

[1] *atu's kį·*, "pot, clock", denoting the hour, is interesting in Catawba semantics. A clay pot rings clear like the stroke of an old clock when tapped on the rim; two o'clock becomes "two pots, or rings", and so on. Even the dove, *itu'sį·* (Texts 27, 50) earns a sobriquet from its call which resembles a stroke of the clock or a pot.

5

mǫtuʾ   *ya'kį'*   *waresa're*   *ya'kį·*   *nųwi·tca'*
when   woman the   sick   woman the   pregnant (lit. "fat, fleshy")

yį·tǝro'   *kį·*   *sabme'hi·we*   *atce'mi·harą'we.*   *yę*   *bo'ye*   *mǫtuʾ*
child   the   poorly will be   a little eat will.   People   know   when

nų'ha'owe   *tǝtci·*   *mǫkųya'we*   *wįt·i·*   *kǝru'*   *kį·*   *we.*
whip us will   cannot   defecate you will   medicine   drink   the   will.

   mo'nų   *ki·*   *ya'*   *kie*   *waresa'*   *yą'tci·we.*   *istci'na*
   Dirt   the   eating   sick   you make will.   Mother my

    ta'smǫsǝką'   *į·tu'*   *ki'*   *mǫbo'kʿhare*   *mi·ra'*   *nata're.*
salt in red [red pepper]   clay   the   in put   more   eat did not.

de'ta   *į·tu*   *tcąta're*   *hadnǫta'ra*   *kusaʾ*   *astare.*
I   clay   eat did   went home did   stop   I did.

FREE TRANSLATION

When making pots some clay may be eaten. It causes worms if much of it is eaten. Clay is not good, it causes sickness. The child will be poorly when born if the woman when sick with pregnancy eats clay. The child will be poorly if it eats a little. When a person knows it he will whip us. You cannot defecate without drinking medicine. Dirt eating will make you sick. My mother put red pepper in the clay and no more was eaten. I used to eat clay but I went home and stopped it.[1]

80. Medicine Blowing by a Catawba Doctor. (III)

   yękwe'   *wį·'ti·*   *ta'howe.*   *tusʿpąse ti*   *wį·tita'hade.*
   Person that   medicine   makes.   Pot   the   medicine make do.

wąsa'   *puʿhade*   *mi'bari·*   *howe.*   *wį·'ti*   *kį'*   *yo'tca*   *puʿhade*
Bamboo   blow do   get better   may.   Medicine   the   you cause   blow do

wikʿha   *mi'bari·*   *howe.*   *puʿhapake're*   *hade*   *bo'boʾhowe*   *mǫtu'.*
heat   get better   may.   Blow up   do   bubble   during.

FREE TRANSLATION

The doctor makes medicine. [He] makes the medicine [in a] pot. Blow [the medicine through a] cane [tube and he will] get better. You blow the medicine and heat (up the sick one and he will] get better. Blow [the medicine and make it] bubble up.

---

[1] For discussion of this practice in various parts of the world, as a pregnancy diet (Africa, South America) and as a habit, see B. Laufer, *Geophagy*. Field Mus. of Nat. Hist. Chicago. Anth. Ser. vol. XVIII, No. 2, 1930.

BLOWING MEDICINE BY THE DOCTOR

The usual practice among the southeastern peoples of blowing through a cane tube into the medicine concoction to charge it with personal power was likewise well known to the Catawba. The herbs, roots or leaves, after being steeped in water in an earthen pot were subjected to this process by the aboriginal practitioner then given to the patient to drink and also blown or sprayed over him by being spouted through the hollow cane pipe after the concoction had been sucked into his mouth. The purpose of this operation, as given by the informant (Sally Brown), was to "steam the sick person and to heat him up". An external as well as an internal one. Unfortunately our information is limited concerning further theories and procedures of this important medicinal doctrine.

The blowing tubes of cane are from 24 inches to 48 inches long and from $1/_2$ to $5/_8$ inch in thickness. They remind one of the blow-gun used in hunting small game. Ordinary cooking bowls were used, the text in which this information was recorded mentions the "pot with legs". At the present time it is usual to see the Catawba steeping herb remedies in small pottery or tin cups.

81. Singing when Giving Medicine.[1] (III)

A.

ya' sak	do' po	ikpo' tąre	yę	wa' resa'	wį·ti	yų' tąre.
Bed	thing	down make	did	person	sick	medicine give did.

i·mǫ' kį·tąre	i'bari	kį'	tą' re	i·mǫ' se	itą' re.	mi'bare
Singing the	did	dancing	the	did	glad did.	Got better

itą' re	sabme'	itą' re.
did	[he who was] poorly	did.

B. (1)

yasá' k	dukhapo' hę'	wį·ti·	miyo' hę'.	imǫ'	tąre	i·ba' rire
Bed	make up	medicine	give.	Sing	did	dance

imosa' tcure.	mi·ba' retąre	sabme' hį·.
get glad very.	Get better did	a [person] who is poorly.

---

[1] In order to compare the diction of the two women who speak Catawba, the text (A) of Sally Brown was read to Mrs. Owl, who repeated it in her own wording (B).

5*

Text A.

When a person was sick, they used to make down a bed and give him medicine. And they used to sing and dance and act glad, they did. Then the ailing one used to get better.

Text B.

[When a person was sick they used to] make up a bed and give [him] medicine. [They used to] sing [and] dance [and act] very glad. [The] person who [was] poorly [would] get better.

82. *Sucking as a Remedial Measure.* (III)

təpa'	yo'tcə'	ka'į'ire	hita°wara'pəre.	wi·tkạ'təro	sa'k	kį·ye
Pin	you use	scratch	breast pain.	Turkey	bone	the

wį'ti·	yo'tca	mətci'ha'	pu'iki·re	it kįt'	ko'wəre
medicine	you use	drop some	blowing in	blood the	comes out

i't kį·.	kamọtu'we	mi'barare	kạ'awe	wa'resa'-
blood the.	Now suck will	get better and	get up will	sick

tcutcuwe.	wį'ti·kį·	kụyi'	yo'tcare	kəru'gəre.
very much will.	Medicine	same	you use	drink to.

Using a pin you scratch the pain in the breast. You use a turkey bone, dropping some of the medicine in and blowing through it as the blood comes out. Now if you will suck the blood, the sick person will get better and also get up completely [recovered]. Some of the same medicine you also use to drink.

83. *Enema for Constipation.* (III)

yẹtụ'kį·	mọkuya're	wį·ti·tụ'kị	o'watca
Person little the	defecate stopped	medicine little the	use

hatạ'de.	wį'ti·	kị·	wik'ha'tcade.	ya'cepis	ki'ye	wạ'sakį
wash do.	Medicine	the	warm make do.	Eel skin	the	cane the

o'tcəde	o'tca	atạ'de.	mi'bari·	howe	asəwạ'	otca'
use do	use	wash do.	Get better	will	very much	using

mi'rotcuwe.
strong too much will be.

[When] baby is constipated use a little medicine for a wash. Warm the medicine. Use an eel skin and cane [tube][1] to rinse out [its intestines]. It will get better, but using too much will be too strong for it.

84. Scratching the Shoulder with Garfish Teeth for Strength. (III)

Yẹsẹbe'hẹna	hadu'tnọyá'	kaįkaịa'we.	yi·hiską' yane
People ancient the	told	scratch we.	Fish head long[2]

kį	hį·ya'p	dəri't'ti	kaįkaįsə'we	yiksə	mọtu'	yəsigri·'we
the	his teeth	my shoulder	scratch I	sore	when	you sore

yətikyu'we	yəmirotcu'we	yəmi·'bari·yuwe.
you strong	you better much	you better you be.

FREE TRANSLATION

The ancient people used to tell us to scratch ourselves. So I scratched my shoulder with teeth from the longheaded fish (the garfish) when I had sores. To do this when you are sore will make you strong and you will be much better.

85. Rules for Gathering Herbs.

When Gathering Herbs Spare Some in the Ground. (III)

nụ'ti·	hatkut‘ha	kaį”hade	tci'pse	kį·ye	nuti·mį'ha.	wį·ti·'-
Sun	sets [side] the	cut do	top	the	sun rise.	Medicine

kuse'	kuse'pi't‘koda	kaį”hode.	iwį·'ti· kį·ye	yamu
vine	stands behind	cut do.	Medicine root the	in water

ke'hade	atcẹ'ha'	mo'notuke'hade	duke'hade	waha'	matciri'k
put do	a little	ground in put do	back put do	not	run away

---

[1] The distribution of the internal syringe in North America appears quite irregular from recorded instances. Hallowell obtained it from the Saulteaux and these occurrences suggested the question to the Catawba with the above result. The Catawba syringe is described by Sally Brown as having a baked clay mouth-piece to the end of the cane tube to be inserted into the rectum. The medicine injected either by an eel skin bulb or another large piece of cane telescoped over the end of the smaller tube.

[2] Specific name for the Gar-fish (Tylosurus marinus).

howe pa'į'howe mǫtu'hawe   tcapako"kutci·we.   du'g mi· howe
may not will be   in will   somewhere else go will.   Back come may

buru'kdugro're   mo'notuke'yu'we.
again back come   in ground when put you will.

FREE TRANSLATION

On the side of the sunset cut the top of the medicine. The medicine vine behind the side of sun rise, cut it. Put the root in water,
and put a little back in the ground, in order that it may not vanish
and there will be no more and that it may not go and get in somewhere else. It will come back again when you put it back in the
ground.

86. *Gathering Medicines and Praying.* (III)

tcawį·ti·kį·'   *mistcu're*   *ya'p*   *kį·*   *desto're*   *yap*
To make medicine   I bring some   tree   the   I peel   tree

pa'sa   wį'ti·   kį·   kərį·howe.   *wa'rəre*
north side medicine the   good will be.   He who never dies [God]

hapi·nų'tci·de'.   *yemehapi·nų'tce'.*
help us do!   By myself help cannot.

FREE TRANSLATION

When going to secure medicine I peel the bark on the north side
of the tree so the medicine will be good. He-who-never-dies (God)
helps me! I cannot help myself.

87. *Gathering Medicines in the Full of the Moon.* (III)

wį'ti·   kį·   ba'ri·   mi·ra'we   asəwǫ'kruga'we.
Medicine   the   better   more will be   a quantity drink will.

wa'ya atu'awe   kruga'we   hakbo'khade   atu'hade kų'waresa'-
Winter save will drink will   up put do   save do give sick

mǫtu'.   an   wį'ti·   kį·ye   yukų'hri'we   atu'a'we
when.   Then   medicine   the   you give have will   save we, will

ake'yade   payuyǫ'wətcu'we.   wi'k   ka'tcəde nų'ti· i'ndəre're
put down do   some sell we will.   Warm   make it   moon   new

nųt'i· pą'hǝre wį·ti· sǝreta'we. ha ki'ye sǝrę'ruwe
moon full medicine pluck will. Digging the to pull it going

te'ki· pade'tcǝtce'.
beware some lose don't.

The medicine will do more good if you drink a quantity of it. Save
it for the winter to drink and put it up to save it for sickness. You
will then have the medicine to give if we put some away, and we
can sell some. It will do more good if it is made warm. Make it
during the new moon or in the full moon pull it up. In digging it
be careful not to lose some of it.

88. Herbal Remedies.[1]

Broom Grass Roots for Backache. (III)

wį·'ti· sǝra'k wį·'ti· sǝre't'hade! wį'ti· sǝra'k hi·sda' wara'p'ha
Root grass root pull up. Root grass back pain the

wį·ti· kį' kǝrį'hǝre.
medicine the good is.

Rattle Box the Catawba Black Drink for Mental Troubles. (III)

wį'ti· sę'sǝre'ha kǝrug'hade. kǝrį'howe yumę'sǝ'
Medicine rattle drink it. May do good your stomach

kǝri''howe. yame'hǝra tcu'awe mi'bari·yuwe.
may do good. Your troubles will not be so much you may be better.

Blunt Manna Grass for Backache. (III)

wį'ti· kį· yąhe" kǝri·'hǝre isda' warup'ha kǝrį'ha.
Root the in water is good [for] back pain the it is good.

ti'ti''hade yehye' mǫtce"hade. wį·ti· kį'ye atu's kį· mǫtcę"hade.
Beat it up water in put it. Medicine the pot the in put it

waha'kusa kutca''hatcade' na'mǝndǝde kǝru'g'hade.
awhile cause it to stay [stand], three times [a day] do drink it.

---

[1] Botanical identities when given are based upon specimens collected in
the field with informants.

Red-Root for Sore Mouth. (III)

tu'ktu[1]   *kəri·kəri'ᵖhəre.*   *wi'ti·*   *kəri'ᵖhəre*   *hi·samy̨ᵖ*   *itci'gəne.*
Red-root   good is.   Root   good is   mouth   child.

tci·tci'samy̨ᵖ   *isi'grəre*   *atą'de!*
Child mouth   sore   wash·do!

China-Berry Medicine for Colds. (III)

hętutcu'   *nostcuwe*ᵖ   *haro'tcuwe*   *kəri̧'*   *ka'tci·we*
China-berry seed   sugar may   boil will   good   make may

itci'gəne   *wi'ti·*   *pi̧'satcu're.*
child   medicine [for] cold severe is.

Pipsissewa for Backache. (III)

wi'ti·   *i·pi·*   *səra'k,*   *wi'ti·*   *səra'k*   *i·pi'həre*   *hisda'*   *warap*
Medicine   fire   flower,   medicine   flower   fire is   back   pain

kəri'kəri'həre.   *wi'ti·*   *ha't*   *mǫtᶜ*   *pa'tki·ye*   *na'mprəri·*
good good is.   Medicine   leaf on ground   flat   both together

mǫbo'kᶜhade   *kəri̧'ᵖhowe.*
in put do.   It good will be.

Red-Root for Sore Nipples. (III)

ta'ktu   *ti·ki̧'ye*   *kəri̧'howe*   *i·ha'sigri·*   *motuᵖ.*
Red-root   root the   good will be   nipples of breast sore when.

taktu'ki̧·   *o'wətca*   *tą'de*   *mi·bari· yu'we*
Red-root the   using   make it [medicine]   better you will be

yi̧·təro'ki̧·   *mi·bari·ho'we.*
person small the   better will be.

Pin Weed for Sores. (III)

wi'ti   *yəhat nuwi̧'həre*   *wi'ti·*   *ti'ti'ᵖhade*   *wi'ti·*
Medicine   leaf-tied   root   beat up thoroughly do   medicine

kaᵖtcide,   *yę'pa'*   *si'gri·.*   *yuyą*ᵖ   *atcemą*   *ke'hade*   *yą'mą'*
make do,   any person sore.   Grease   a little   in put do   water in

ke'hade   *ha'ro*   *kəri̧'həre.*   *wi'ti·kəri̧'*   *katcu'we.*
put do   boil   nicely.   Medicine good   make very will.

---

[1] The word is pronounced *ta'ktuwi* by Mrs. Owl.

Black Locust for a Beverage. (III)

yapətę́   *kį·*   *wi·rą́ həre*   *ədreyą́*   *kəruga' we*   *kustą́*
Tree flat [pod]   the   eat we   beer   drink we may   bread

hị·   *hagrą́ həre*   *kəruga' we.*
the   together put is   drink we will.

Milkweed Medicine for Snake-bite. (III)

səra' k   *wita' səre*   *ya' tcuk͓ha*   *wį'ti·*   *kərį'həre*   *ya*   *wį·ti·.*
Flower   milk   snake bite   medicine   good is   snake medicine.

wi·ta's kį·   *owatcaᵖ*   *yę́ paˀ*   *tcuk hi·k wa' we*   *mi'bari*   *huwe.*
Milk   the   using   person's foot   bite kills may   get better   may.

ya' kį·   *tcuk͓dawa' riwe.*   *ya*   *sigri·həreᵖ.*
Snake the   bite somewhere go die will.   Snake poisonous is.

Mole's Foot and Sharp-Root for Baby Teething. (III)

wapuᵖ   *hi·paᵖ*   *kaįˀi'we,*   *itci' gəneˀ*   *pakta' wəho' we.*
Mole   his foot   cut off may,   child   around neck put may

hį·ya' p   *kaį i' we*   *kərį·*   *ho' we.*   *wį'ti·*   *hi·tci'həre*   *yę́ pakta-*
his teeth   cut will   good   is.   Medicine   sharp   persons neck

weho' we.   *unia' tᶜ*   *deya' səde*   *kaį*   *tǫ' we*   *tci·aˀ*   *kaįkaį'*
put may.   Then   string it do   cut   teeth   make   cut it up

pakta' wəhəde   *wį'ti·*   *hi·tcį·həre*   *kəru' k͓həde*   *nosurę́ᵖ.*   *ki·ye*
around neck put   medicine   sharp   drink it do   lives.   The

yę təro'   *wa'saᵖtcure*   *hį' mǫtuᵖ*   *mǫ' sərepəre*
person little   sick make very   sleeps when   scares it.

baresa're   *hi'mare*   *kərį'tcaˀ.*
It gets better   sleep   good makes it.

Tobacco to Cure Horses. (III)

į'pa   *wi·tsəgwą́ i·*   *wa'resaˀ*   *kərį'həre.*   *mi'bare*   *ho' we.*
Tobacco   horse   sick   good is.   [He] get better   will.

haro' tcade   *mi·ro' tcade,*   *wutepi'*   *mǫ*   *bu' k͓hade*   *mǫtcę́' hade*
Boil do   strong make it,   bottle   in   put do   in pour do

kəruk͓hatcide.
drink cause do.

Bear-Root for Rheumatism and Fever. (III)

ni·ha′g   wara′p‘hǝre¹   kru′g   ki·   yehi·ye′   kǝrę″aha′re.   nǝmę″
My body   pain   drink   the   water   good not.   Bear

wi′ti² hį·   wi′ti· kį·   ho′tcu we   hapi·ǫtci· we   kunitcu′hare
medicine   root   use may   good be   good so (quickly)

wi·tca′sǝtcu′we.³   nusa′pwaraptcu′we⁴   wi′khatcuri′sǝre.⁵
chill I much may.   My bone pain much may   hot wet I.

Devil's Shoestring for Rheumatism. (III)

yę   mbara″   wi·ya′hawa″   yap‘ha   wǝte′   tug bu′k   hade
Man   bad   string the   tree leaf   moccasin   in put   do

mi·bari·   yu′we   yǝhagyo′   wara′p‘hatcure.
better   you be   your body flesh pain much.

Heart-Leaf for Heart and Stomach Trouble. (III)

"pi′tca"   ha′hore   wi′tina   ni·ta′wara′p hatcu′re⁶
"Pitcher"   leaves come   medicine my   my heart pain much

kǝrę″tcure.
good very.

Adam and Eve Root for Boils. (III)

yę   yaske″   kį·ye   ya   aske″   kį·ye   ya′   migra′ha   wį′ti
Man   first   the   woman   first   the woman   with the   root

kį·   wi′ti   kį′ti·.   ki·tia′we   si′gri kį·⁷   pa′a′we   mi·bari·ho′we
the root   the.   Beat we   boil the   powder we   better be

hiskǫ′ kį· ho′we.   diskǫ′   warap   hatcu′re.
head   the be.   My head   pain   much.

---

¹ Term denotes fever.
² Bear-root.
³ Denotes chills and ague.
⁴ Denotes ague and rheumatism.
⁵ Denotes sweating.
⁶ Term denoting heart disease.
⁷ Denotes also "something spoiled, decayed, salty."

Sour-Wood for Female Complaints.[1] (III)

yαp	*hitaᵖare*	*hi·tatcu're*	*atce*	*beᵖsəwe.*		*ya'*	*ki·*
Tree	sour	sour very	little	bite (taste) I.		Woman	the

waresa'retcure[2]	*i·hi·ye*	*tci·ha*	*bo'k*	*hade*	*ihi·ye'ti*	*tug*	*bo'k*
sick very	water	cold the	put	do	water the	in	put

hade.	*kru'g*	*hade*	*mi'bari*	*ho'we.*
do.	Drink	do	better	be.

Bloodroot for Horse Tonic. (III)

wį·ti	*səkα*ᵖ	*yira'tcide.*		*yi'ra'tci*	*ti²ti²de*	*səmi'*
Root	red	dry powder do.		Dry powder	crush do	crush

hatcade	*witsəgwaį'*	*ya*	*kru'gʻhowe*	*nǫ'we*	*tcu'we.*
make do	horse	your	drink may	fat	very be.

Water-Root for Backache. (III)

wį·'ti	*ya'mubahę*ᵖ	*yę*	*səda'ha*	*wį'ti*	*hi*ᵖ	*kusa'*	*yə-*
Root	in water the	person	back the	root	the	stand	your

səda'	*wara'pʻha*	*kərįᵖhəre.*	*wi'ti·ka*	*tcakrug a'we.*
back	pain the	good.	Root some	cause drink we.

Daddy-Long-Legs in Dough Swallowed for Chills. (III)

tcα	*suk*	*se*ᵖ	*hį'pa*	*įpəre'tcure*	*kuspa'tə*
Insect	house	old (spider)	his leg	long very[3]	corn meal the

təba'rəre.	*kəru'gsuwe*	*wi·tca'*	*pasa're.*
dough.	Swallow I	chills	none I.

Rattlesnake Skin Bound on Head for Headache. (III)

Ya'	*swα*		*ki*	*pis*	*isto'həre*	*hiska'nərehəre*
Snake	chief	(rattlesnake)	the	skin	skin	one's head tie

---

[1] Knowledge of the efficacy of this remedy was derived from suggestion in a dream, by Sam Blue. When he tried it out he found it beneficial.

[2] Term denoting female complaints.

[3] Specific name for Daddy-long-legs.

hiskạ'warap[1]	*kəɾę⁰həre.*	*tapəkę'*	*kəɾę⁰*	*tcu*	*we*	*tuki'ye*
one's head pain	good for.	Fiddle	good	very	be	button

tuki	*ki't*	*hade.*
off	take	do.

Snapping-Turtle Heart Swallowed for Long Life. (III)

kaya'	*skạtəro'*	*hitawę⁰*	*kəɾu'gəre*	*waˤra'*	*kane'həre,*	*wɔ⁰na*
Terrapin	head big	his heart	swallow	live	long time,	live

kane'həre	*i·wa're*	*si'gri·re*	*sigri·tcu're.*
long time	die	hard	hard very.

Ball-Root for Sores. (III)

wi'ti	*ki·*	*warupˤha*	*ki·*	*haro'səde*	*nu'yạ*	*ki·*	*ha'rosəde'*
Root	the	round	the	boil do	grease (salve)	the	boil do

yəhagyo'	*wɔ·'wəde*	*yę'pasi'grəre*	*mi·ba'rəre.*
your body flesh	rub do	person any boils	better is.

Pennyroyal for Colds. (III)

sụ'wə	*ki·*	*wi'ti·*	*ki·*	*səre'thade*	*haro'tcade*	*kəɾę⁰howe*	*tci'-*
Smell	the	root	the	pull up do	boil cause do	good be	cold

wepˤha	*hi·we*	*hitcəwa'tcade.*
catch the	may	sweat cause do.

Holly Leaves for Measles. (III)

wɔ·tatcá'ne	*i'satcure*[2]	*i·sigri'həre*	*yapˤha*
He has measles	badly	sores	tree leaves

hitce	*he⁰*	*wi'ti·*	*ki·*	*ta akru'g awe.*
sharp	(holly tree)	the	medicine	the	make drink we.

yę'	*sębe'*	*wi'ti·*	*ti*	*kru'gəre.*
People	ancient	medicine	a	drink.

Cause of Diarrhea and Star-Grass Cure. (III)

turi'ye	*hę⁰*	*turi·tci'ne*	*hę⁰*	*mọ'hi·ya'*	*yawe*	*itme'-*
Apple	the [and]	plum	the	diarrhea	you may	blood

---

[1] Equivalent for headache.

[2] Specific name given for measles.

mǫhi·ya'tcuwe.
diarrhea much may.

wą'sahawəne
Cane leaves (star grass)

yehi·ye'
water [in]

tug buk a'we. krug a'we mǫ'wokwę tcu're¹ huka't kusa'-
in put we. Drink we diarrhea much now stop

mi·ba'ri·tare i·t'me'həre kahate".
better make blood at once, indeed.

Aider-Tag for Constipation in Children. (III)

du'kəri' ha yę təro' waresa're mǫtu' mǫ'wo kį·
Next and the person small sick when diarrhea the

kusa"hatəre.² hi·tu'kį wa'p'tu ho'tcere kərę"howe.
stop. His little the alder-tag uses good may.

Yellow-Root for Jaundice. (III)

wį'ti nusę" wį·ti kį' ha'rowe kəruga'we imba're i'we
Root yellow root the boil drink we get better may

yę' habe'həre.
man looks poorly.³

Bear Grass for Skin Diseases. (III)

nęmę" səra'k kį· wį'ti· kį yəhagyo'pis wawa'wəde.
Bear grass the root the your body flesh skin rub on do.

mi·bari· yo'we wį'ti kərę"həre nąpəre tų' hi· tcuwi'rere
Better you be medicine good two small many

mi·ro kərę" yəwe kru'gha da hopi'de. do'pətcuti·
more good you be drink go lie down do. Something different

ǫ'wətcade nəmę" kį· səra'k wi·d·yo'ki· sugbu'kpuka'we
use cause do bear the grass animal meat the on put we

ha'pərą'a'we.
hang up we.

---

¹ Specific name for diarrhea.
² Specific name for constipation.
³ This term denotes jaundice.

Broom Grass Roots for Backache

Root grass, pull up the root. Root grass is the backache medicine. It is good!

Rattle Box the Catawba Black Drink for Mental Trouble.

The rattle medicine drink it. It may do good to your stomach; may do it good. Your troubles will not seem so serious. You may be better.

Blunt Manna Grass for Backache

Water-root is good for backache. It is good. Beat it up and put it in water. Put the medicine in the pot and cause it to stand a while. Drink it three times a day.

Red-Root for Sore Mouth.

Red-root is good indeed. It is a good medicine root for the mouth of a child. When the little one's mouth is sore, wash with it.

China-Berry Medicine for Colds.

China-berry (Melia azedarach) seed boiled well with sugar will make a good medicine for a child with a severe cold.

Pipsissewa for Backàche.

The medicine [known as] fire-flower, or medicine-flower (Chimaphila umbellata), for backache is very, very good. The medicine flatleaf, (Asarum arifolia) put in together with it. It will be good.

Red-Root for Sore Nipples.

The roots of red-root will prove good when nipples become sore. Using the red-root make it up into medicine. You will be better and the little child will be better.

Pin Weed for Sores.

The medicine tie-leaf[1] root beat up thoroughly; make into medicine for anyone with sores. Put in a little grease and put it in water to boil well. It will make a good medicine.

---

[1] Identity of the plant is *Lechia* (sp ?). The Catawba name is derived from the deeply indented leaves.

Black Locust for a Beverage.

The flat (pod) tree[1] (Black Locust) we eat, and we can make beer of it, putting it together with bread and drinking it.

Milkweed Medicine for Snake-Bite.

Milk-flower[2] is good medicine for snake-bite. For snake medicine the milk (juice) is used. Rub it on the person's foot, the foot where the snake bite is, it may cause death. If it does get better the snake that bit (the person) will go away somewhere and die. The snake is poisonous.

Mole's Foot and Sharp-Root for Baby Teething.

If a mole's foot is cut off and put around a child's neck it will cut its teeth well. Sharp-medicine[3] may also be put around a person's neck. Then string it, cutting up the sharp-medicine into pieces, around the neck for teething, and drink it. The little-people[4] (dwarfs) cause hives, making the child frightened when it sleeps, by scaring it. When it recovers it permits it to sleep well.

Tobacco to Cure Horses.

Tobacco is good for a sick horse. He will get better. Boil it well, make it strong, put it in a bottle, pour it in and make him drink it.

Bear-Root for Rheumatism and Fever.

For body-pain (rheumatism) do not drink water. The bear medicine root may be good, very much good for my severe chills (and fever) when I am hot with severe bone-pain (ague).

Devil's Shoestring for Rheumatism.

The bad-man's (Devil's) string (Devil's Shoe-String, Tephrosia virginiana) leaves put in your shoe to get better from pain in the flesh of the body (fever).

Heart-Leaf for Heart and Stomach Trouble.

Pitcher leaves (Asarum arifolia) are my medicine for severe pain in the heart (heart disease). They are very good.

---

[1] *Robinia pseudacacia*, so named in Catawba after the shape of its pod.

[2] Asclepias (sp. ?).

[3] Herb unidentified.

[4] "Wild people".

Adam and Eve Root for Boils.

The first man (Adam) and first woman (Eve) root (Aplectrum hyemale) is the medicine. We beat it up and boil the powder for boils and pain in the head. My head aches badly!

Sour-Wood for Female Complaints.

The sour-tree (Oxydendron arboreum) is very sour tasting when I bite it. When a woman is very sick put some of it in cold water, and she drinks it to get better.

Bloodroot for Horse Tonic.

Red-root (Sanguinaria canadensis) dry and make into powder and crush it up. When it is crushed up, if your horse drinks it, it may make him quite fat.

Water-Root for Backache.

Water-root (identity uncertain, ?Arnica acaulis) or the medicine for the person's back, is good for a pain in the back. We make (the sufferer) drink some of it.

Daddy-Long Legs in Dough Swallowed for Chills.

The old-house insect (spider) whose leg is very long (daddy-long-legs) rolled in corn meal dough. I swallow so that I will have no chills.

Rattlesnake Skin Bound on the Head for Headache.

The snake-chief (Banded rattlesnake) skin (should be) taken off and tied on one's head for pain in the head to relieve it. It is very good for (the tone of) a fiddle if you put inside it a rattlesnake's rattle, i. e., "take off its button".

Snapping-Turtle Heart Swallowed for Long Life.

The big-head terrapin's (Snapping-turtle) heart swallow to live a long time, to live a very long time, and to die very, very hard.

Ball-Root for Sores.

The round-root (Psoralea pedunculata) boil, and boil the grease (salve) from it. Rub it on the flesh when a person has boils to make him better.

Pennyroyal for Colds.

The smell-root (Hedeoma pulegioides) pull up and bring to boiling. It will do good when one catches cold, causing to sweat.

Holly Leaves for Measles.

He who has measles badly has sores. Sharp-leaf tree (Ilex opaca) leaves made into medicine we drink. This was an ancient peoples' drink.

Cause of Diarrhea and Star-Grass Cure.

Eating the apple and the plum may cause dysentery, you may even have bloody dysentery. Star-grass-leaves (Aletrias farinosa) we put in water. We drink it for dysentery when bad. It will relieve and stop the blood at once.

Alder-Tag for Constipation in Children.

Next when a child is sick with dysentery stop (constipation). Using a little alder-tag may do good.

Yellow-Root for Jaundice.

The yellow-root (Xanthorrhiza apiifolia) we boil and drink to get better when we look poorly (have jaundice).

Bear Grass for Skin Disease.

The bear grass (Yucca filamentosa) root rub on your body flesh to got better. Two small pieces or more are good for the medicine. You will get better if you drink it and go lie down. We use the bear grass for another purpose, we use it to put meat on to hang it up.

PART IV

SOCIAL CUSTOMS

DANCES.

89. The Catawba Round Dance. (I)

yḝ'ye	kata'pa	hị	iba'rihę⁰	ara'dəret.	ibari·	ha'
People	Catawba	the	dance	long ago.	Dance	they

ni·tcehę⁰	katapaˁti'	yḝ'ye	terako⁰	ị·pi' wi·a⁰	ehe⁰	i'bare
so did	Catawba	the	people	outside fire	some	make dance

umpa'tcehę⁰.	i'baria'hahe⁰	ye'musi·kịnt'	ibari·a'hahe⁰.	wi·tca'wa
around.	Dance lead	man old the	dance lead.	Night

iba'rihe⁰	wi·tca'wa	terarahe⁰	ya'bəri	ibara'hę⁰.
dance [they]	night	half (mid-night)	daylight	dance not.

ye'musikint mu'hịę⁰	a'gərapti	haga'rihę⁰	yémbri·tce⁰	ni·te'm.
Man old the sing	other the	join with	man	all.

ya	katara'hę⁰	ya'kęnt'	dagosa'hahe⁰.	itci'gni
Woman	the with (partner)	woman the	behind stand.	Child

pa'ị·ha'hę.
none.

FREE TRANSLATION

The Catawba people danced long ago. The Catawba people, they made a fire outside and danced around it. The dance was led by an old man. They danced at night until the night was half over (mid-night). They did not dance when it was daylight. The old man would sing and all the other men would join with him. The women stand behind their partners. Children (did not dance).

90. The Catawba Horse Dance. (I)

wi·tsagwạị⁰	iba'rihę⁰	iba'ri	tcute tcahę⁰.	papi'tcini·	ibarihę⁰
Horse	dance	dance	different.	About ten	dance

hadihi'	ina'	dugəro'hę⁰.	ni'tem	ya'	katara'hę⁰	ibari'	ị·pi'ki
forward	go	back.	All	woman	partner	dance	fire the

ina′ he°   *ani′ du′gərohę°*.   *yembri′tce*   *mei·mo′ hę°*.   *atci′ kpe*
go toward   then back go.   Man   alone sing.   Step

wą′ tcα′tcohę°.   *ya′ kęnt*   *mitce′*   *tcakwa′ hę°*   *ya′ kęnt*
jump fast.   Woman the   don't   touch [them]   woman the

mitce′ mowa′ hę°.
don't   sing.

FREE TRANSLATION

The horse dance is different. About ten dance forward and then go back. Every woman has a partner and they dance toward the fire and then retreat. Only the men sing. They step and jump fast. The woman do not touch the men. The women do not sing.

91. The Wild Goose Dance. (III)

eha′ su′ re   *i·ba′ re.*   *suko*   *i·ba′ rəra*   *yemusa′*
Goose wild   dance.   House a   dance together   chair

naipa′ tca   *i·baretcuwi°tare*   *sų′ti·kəre′be*   *tą′ yotca*   *sugi·pa′ tca.*
around going   dance much   door open   going out   house around.

tąko′   *ya*   *ikəba′ tase′ tca*   *sų′ti·*   *tatki′*   *kəba′*   *mono′ kəba*
Door yard   you   sweep   clean   door   front the   sweep   dirt swept

tą′ bokˤhəre.   *i·ba′ retcu′ re*   *nǫde*   *su′ grore.*   *i·yą′*
away from.   Dance hard   turn back   in house come.   Whiskey

[*i·yąhəre*]   *kru′ grere*   *ni·te′m*   *yąsa′ re*   "*yo′+*   *ho+*   *i′ho+*   *yeki·-*
          drink   all   get drunk   "yo   ho   i· hȯ   yeki·-

ya wa ne we ha yu yo wa hye+   *de′ hanesəta′ no.*"
yu wa ne we ha yu yo wa hye+ I can do this way [by motions]."

do′ ka   *hadu′ dare*   *i·yę′ i·ba′ re*   *hadu′ da ki·*   *hamuse′ kǫhi·re*
We   say this   Indian dance   the way of saying   we are happy

ya   *musi′.*
old   women.

FREE TRANSLATION

The Wild Goose dance. In a house they dance together going around a chair considerably, out of the open door and around the house. The door yard is swept clean and from in front of the door the dirt is all swept away. Dancing hard they turn back and come into the house. They drink whiskey and all get drunk. "*Yo + ho + i'ho + yeki· ya wa ne we ha yu yo wa hye + de'hanesəta'no.*" We say this in the Indian dance manner of expressing that we are happy, the old women [and the old men, we dance together.]

92. *The Bear Dance.* (III)

nəmę"	*ba'rəre*	*i·mǫ'tu*	*i·ba'rəre*	*wa'de*	*kį'ye*	*mǫ*	*səre"*
Bear	dance	when	dance	gourd	the	when	rattling

səre"howe	*i·ba'retcure.*	*yę*	*migra"*	*kį·*	*ba'retcure*	*wat'katu"*
may make	dance hard.	Man	great	the	dance hard	feathers

kayoi'we	*yę'ksa*	*o'wətca'*	*kayo'wəde.*	*yapkę'*	*mǫ*	*nų'wi·hade*
waving	in hand	using	wave them.	Calf-leg	on	tie

wa'de	*kį·ye*	*kaha"atcu'we.*
gourd	the	laugh much.

FREE TRANSLATION

When dancing the Bear Dance (they) dance when rattling the gourd (to make them) dance hard. The chief dances waving feathers, carrying them waving in his hand. On the calf of the leg tie the gourd (rattle) and laugh much.

MARRIAGE.

93. *On Marriage of Close Kin.* (III)

yę	*kį'i·sahəre*	*agi·pe'tce'.*	*kərį'hare.*	*yę*	*kę'sa're*
Persons	close kin	marry do not.	Not good.	Persons	distant kin

akpi'de.	*kərį·'hare.*	*dopətcu'ksigri'*
marry do.	Not good it is.	Something very mean [spoiled]

tə'paya'wəre	*itci'gni·*	*na*	*kərį·'wa'we.*	*e"mogrə*
might happen	[to] children	my	not good might be.	Minds

kərį'hawe.
not good might be.

FREE TRANSLATION

Persons of close kin, do ye not marry! It is not good. Persons of distant kin, marry ye! (otherwise) it is not good. Something might happen to produce spoiled (defective) children, if I did so it might not be good. Their minds might not be good.

DEATH.

94. Burial Beneath the House, Giving the Ghost a Drink of Water and the Watch for Three Days after Death. (III)

iyę́ye   sę⁰   i·wa′remọtu⁰   su′kha   pugbu′kəre   mo′notuke
Indians ancient die when   house under   put   ground in

kị́   ya′su   ke′bəre   mọ′notuke′həre   nuntu′re.   wi·yi′pi
the   grave   dug   in ground put   house corner. Right there

wa′rere kot⁽pi yi′pi·   mo′notuke′re.   yap   na′mənere   omo′notukewa′
die   there   in ground put.   Day   three   in ground bury

hịda′¹   kị·ye   duko′we   yęhị·ye′   kru′gowe.   yehi·ye′²
his spirit the   back come may water the drink may.   Water

hị·da′   kru′kha   tci·na′səna   ho′we.   mo′notukəe′we   yę́wa
his spirit drink   shake   may. In ground bury may people

ni·te′mp   imakịka′we.   ị′pa   hị·   ya′katcide   hitca′wa
all   keep awake may. Fire the   keep light do   night

na′mini·we   i′makị·ta′re.   dure⁰harą́we   yap   na′məne   i·makị·
three will   keep awake.   Eat not may   day   three   wake the

dəta′ka   du⁽rą́we.   itus   kị́   hug   bu′k   hade   kus
after awhile   eat not may.   Pot   the   down put   do   corn

tą́t⁽   tug bu′k hade ị′pi·   pis   kị·ye′həre
baked (bread)   in put do fire   skin (ember) the (when out)

itus kị·   mọbu′khade.   ya′tci·bu′khade   sų́ti itci′gəne'.   yi′ksa'
pot the around put do. Ashes throw do   door children.   Your hand

pu⁽hade   yę́wa   kato′newe   waha′te.   tcirik′ha′we
blow on do   person dead bother may   if not.   Run away we

hate′.
right now!

FREE TRANSLATION

The ancient Indians, when anyone died, dug a grave in the ground underneath the corner of the house and put him in the ground. They buried him the ground near where he died. Three days after he was buried it was thought that his spirit would come back and drink water. If his spirit drinks the water will ripple. Before

---

¹ Denotes also "shadow, picture, ghost".
² Note how nazalization varies in sentence dictation.

they buried him in the ground, all the people would keep awake. For three nights they would keep the fire and lights. They could not eat for three days while they were awake (watching). After a while they could eat. In the pot they put corn bread and put embers all around the pot. The children threw ashes out of the door. It is said that they would take ashes in their hands and blow them on the dead person so that his spirit would not bother them. We run away right now!

PERSONAL NARRATIVES.

95. Mrs. Owl's Recollection of Going to Church. (I)

*di·təro'sa mọtu*ᵇ		*eskatre'*	*ya'psənda'kwą'hę*ᵓ
I young	when	clear complexion (white man)	preach had

*monuya'ni·hę*ᵓ.	*uniatᶜ*	*yę'yet*	*ya'psəndaᵓ*	*mona'hę.*	*unia't*ᶜ
mile one.	Then	people	preaching	go.	Then

*e'skatrę*ᵓ	*eᵓehę*ᵓ.	*uni'k*ᶜ	*tərą'bagᵓ*	*eti'rię*ᵓ	*hakutce*ᵇ
white man	not like it.	Then	out put	it is said	afterwards

utkani·tco'ha mọtuᵓ		*eskatrę'*ᵓ	*kint*	*waresa'heᵓ.*	*unia't*ᶜ
sometime	very in	white man	the	mortally sick.	Then

utaᵇ	*yę*	*a'gərap,*	*"udwapke*ᵇ	*dugəraᵓ*	*yęye'kəre'*
he said	people	other,	"Tell not	again	people those

*tərą'bagwotce*ᵇ	*de'rateᵓ*	*unani·ya't*	*kuni·ya'hari."*
out put do not	like I [did]	tried those	good not is."

FREE TRANSLATION

When I was young, there was a white man preacher a mile (from my home). Then the Indian people would go to church. And the white man did not like it, it is said. After a while the white man (preacher) was taken mortally sick. Then he said to the other people, "Let it be told never again to put those Indian people out (of church) like I tried to do. It is not good."

96. Famine Time. (III)

mono	*ną'prəre*	*iswąᵇ*	*korą'tcure*	*kusəri're.*	*ani*	*dure'*
Year	two	river	rose	corn planting.	Then	work

katca're	*duka'ka*	*mona'hrəre*	*asəmi'ka*	*mona'hrəre.*
made nothing	hungry the	nothing have	naked the	nothing have.

eskatrę'	*kərį' hapi· nu'ntcere.*	*nite'mp*	*yę kərį'-*

Clear skin [white man] good help bring.   All people good

wəhi·we	*yę'ye*	*pə*	*si'ahrəre*	*do'pahani'.*	*inu'-*

like may be Indian persons poor something which give. We are

hawoa're.

thankful.

FREE TRANSLATION

For two years the river has risen over the corn planting. Then no work was done, hungry time, have nothing, nakedness having nothing. Good white people bring us help. May all good people be like that to give poor Indians something. We are thankful.

97. Catawba Poverty. (III)

yę'pa	*si·ye'səre.*	*wate'pai̧'saha're.*	*wate'*	*mǫsəra'psərə*

Person poor am I. Shoe not I have. Shoe when I put on

na'musa'ratcure.	*yę'pa'*	*sənų'tcwi'həre.*	*yęyę'*	*waᵖhəre*

I am very glad. Somebody money much has. Man rich

sənųᵖmi·ni·de.

money give me do.

FREE TRANSLATION

A poor person am I. I do not have even a shoe. When I put a shoe on I am very glad. Somebody who has much money, some rich man, do give me money!

PART V

INDUSTRIES AND OCCUPATIONS

98. How the Catawba Make Pots and Pipes. (1)

itu's   ta'sə   namu'rihę⁰   į'nto   dahę⁰   į·nto'ᵎ   hi'mi'   sərihę⁰   itus-
Pot   make   I desire   clay   I dig   clay   beat   I do   pot

ta'sərehe.   į·to⁰   daparą⁰   itus kį'   dakatcahe⁰   i·nto⁰   kį'   umparą'
make I.   Clay   I roll   pot the   I make [it]   clay   the   rolled out

ki'ye   sa'gwoha   ǫnda'tcehę⁰   hapki·sa'hę⁰   datcehę⁰.   tci'm   odotca⁰
that   on top   I make it   up I raise   I make.   Shell   use

daka'wahę⁰.   unia't   yarą⁰   ǫnda'tcehę⁰   ya'raha⁰   hayatᶜ   tcwak-
I scrape.   Then   dry   I make it   dry   when   straight

tca'   datcehę⁰   hi·ᵎ   usa'hǫtcehę⁰.   yara'   mǫtu't ᶜ   datəri'rehę⁰.
and even   I make   handle   I put on.   Dry   when   I rub it.

paną⁰səmǫtu't ᶜ   namu'rehę⁰   yanapi's   dowatca⁰   namu're   ni·te'm
Done   when   I burn [them]   tree bark   I use   I burn   all

į·pi'   ki   pą⁰ihę⁰   yanapi's   sakpą'sahę⁰.   itus kį'
fire   the   turn [face down]   tree bark   on top I put.   Pot   the

namu'   mǫtu't   yanapi's   tca'gikəre'   mǫtu⁰   hawu't ka'hę'
burn   when   tree bark   touch well   when   black make

yį·yantci'   mǫtutᶜ   nuyą'   ontce'rahę⁰   sinųmį'tcį·ᵎsəhę⁰.   wami·su'ta'
ready   when   sell   do I   money earn I.   Pipe

ta'a·səhę⁰   daparą⁰   waru'hantca'   warą'ŋksəhę'.   wamisu'   keb   odo'tca
make I   I roll   round   bend I [it].   Pipe   borer   use

ke'bsəhę⁰   simpa'   odotca⁰   ke'bsəhe   yįye'   hiską⁰   ta'asəhę'.
bore I [it]   knife   use   bore I [it]   person   head   make I.

paną'səmu'nt   nuya'ntcehę⁰   dəpę'   sinų'təri   mura'hę'.
Done when   sell cause   one   money little (25 cents)   worth.

itus   itcuti⁰   ta'asəhę⁰   dəpę'   tusəpase'hį⁰   dapəsi'wi·   itus
Pot   different   make I   one   pot foot cut   the   flower   pot

tərowa⁰ ra'ahę⁰. ni·wori'ri mǫtut⁰ itu's pe'tę ta'·'ehę' i·yęye' ti
little besides. I young when pot flat make people the

iskatrę̨́ iya⁰ nuyą⁰ wahę⁰ wi·ta's matcę⁰ehę⁰.   utke'
white woman sell [them] milk pour in.   Way far

du'kuko⁰ kata'pa yakę́ ta⁰ehę⁰ nuyą́ otcehę⁰.   iskatrę̨́
back ago Catawba many for make sell do.   White-

i·ya' ka u'dihę' wi·ta's yąŋk sukpi·⁰ hap⁰ko kuni'itirie·'.
woman the say milk grease top up good it is said.

i·nto⁰ ya ki' motu' utkani (hę⁰) duko'hę⁰ huka't i·nto'ya'su'
Clay dug the when long time back now clay-hole

patki'hę⁰. i·nto'kint ya mǫtut⁰ u'nti tug⁰bagi·hę⁰ yudugina'hę⁰
big. Clay the dug when bag in put take home go

ǫnto⁰ yasu' mona'mǫtut⁰ kųye' darasa'hę⁰. uke'tca mųtu'
clay hole ground in there noon-time. Leave when

nuwa'nti·ra motu't⁰ manu kị' dug⁰ba'gihę⁰ yasu kị' pą⁰ i·hę⁰.
depart when earth the back in put hole the fill up.

uni⁰k⁰ nuwa'nti·hę (dugi·tcahę⁰).
Then leave (home go).

FREE TRANSLATION

When I desire to make pots I dig the clay. I beat the clay when I make pots. I roll the clay when I make pots. When the clay is rolled out I raise [build] it up to the top. Using a shell, I scrape it. Then when it is dry I make it straight and even and make a handle which I put on. When it is dry I rub it. When they are done I burn [them]. When I burn them I use tree bark. I burn them all in the fire turned face downward, and I put tree bark on top. When the pots are burning the tree bark touches them and makes them black. When they are ready I sell them to earn money. When I make pipes I roll [the clay] round and bend [it]. I use a pipe borer and bore it, using a knife I bore [make] a person's head. When it is done I sell it to make a little money, only twenty-five cents worth. I make different kinds of pots. One pot with flowers cut on the foot, besides little pots. When I was young I made a flat pot and a white woman sold them to the people to pour milk in. A long time ago the Catawba made many [pots] to sell. The white woman said that the milk grease came up to the top well, it is said.

For a long time back clay has been dug, now the hole is big. When the clay is dug put it in a bag to take home. Put it in the ground in the clay hole until you leave at noon-time. When you depart put some earth back in the hole to fill it up. Then leave, go home.

99. How Cane Baskets are Made. (I)

wasa'p^c	*ta^ⁿehę̨^ⁿ*	*mora'mǫtut*	*i'swᾳtak*	*ina'hę̨^ⁿ*	*wᾳsa'*
Basket	make	want when	river valley	go	cane

kᾳ'ehę̨^ⁿ	*tcayi'tcα'.*	*dugi·na'hę̨'*	*wᾳsa'*	*ki· sę̨^ⁿihę̨^ⁿ,*
cut	much do.	Back again go [bring back]	cane	the split.

wasa'p^c	*katcǝhę̨^ⁿ*	*tcoyi'*	*tcǝhę̨^ⁿ.*	*yę̨'pa*	*hᵢ̨*	*hata'*	*nuyᾳ'wahę̨^ⁿ*
Basket	make	many	very.	Person	the	many	buys

wasap^c	*ta^ⁿe*	*mǫtu^ⁿ.*	*yapkaᵢ̨'e*	*kida'*	*hatcα^ⁿ*	*isto'hye'*	*wi'yata^ⁿehę̨^ⁿ*
basket	make when.	Tree cut	down cause	bark	thong make

ǫwǝtcα^{ⁿ·}	*nuwi'yǝhę̨^ⁿ*	*kate'wohę̨^ⁿ.*	*watka^ⁿse'he'e^ⁿ*	*ᵤ^ⁿtcα·*	*hisu^ⁿ*	*hᵢ̨·*
using	tie you	on edge.	White oak splints	use	handle	a

katcǝhę̨^ⁿ.	*waru'pis*	*ǫwǝtcα^ⁿ*	*hawo't*	*katcǝhę̨^ⁿ.*	*wayu'k*	*te^ⁿ*
make.	Walnut bark	using	black	make.	Puccoon[1]	root

owotcǝhę̨^ⁿ	*sik^c*	*katcǝhę̨^ⁿ*	*wᾳsa'sę̨'he'e^ⁿ.*
using	red	make	cane splints.

FREE TRANSLATION

When you want to make baskets, go down to the river bottom and cut much cane. Bring back a quantity of split cane. Make many baskets. Many persons will buy the baskets when they are made. Cut down a tree to get the bark for a thong to bind the rim [of the basket]. Use white-oak splints to make a handle. By using walnut bark a black dye, and puccoon root a red dye is made [to color] the cane splints.

100. Tanning Process. (III)

wǝde^ⁿ	*de*	*histo'de.*	*wǝde'pisǝre*	*yatci'*	*hę̨^ⁿ*	*ta'sǝhę̨^ⁿ*
Cow	the	skin do.	Cow hide	ashes	the [and]	salt the

sagpukhu'k^chade.	*wǝde^ⁿ*	*ki·*	*hiskᾳ'tuksa*	*kᵢ̨·*	*du'ri·de*
on put do.	Cow	the	head-in-fluid [brains]	the	take out do

---

[1] Blood-root (Sanguinaria) famous among the eastern Indians.

ǫ'watca	*kitki't hade*	*pitse'hǝre.*	*mo'no*	*sa'g*	*puk*	*hade*	
using	rub do	outside.	In ground	in	put	do	

mo'notuke'hę"	*yap*	*pa'rpǝre.*	*mo'no*	*sat*	*du'ra*	*de*	*hise'*
in ground put	day	four.	Ground	out	take	do	hair

sǝret'ho'we	*atą'de*	*tere'si'hatcade.*	*uni·a't'*	*haprą'hade*
clear off be	wash it do	clear hair make do.	Then	up hang do

yap o'wǝtca	*tce'tcetcade.*	*ya'ra'*	*aha*	*kǝrę"*	*howe*	*da*	*nuyę"*	*ǫtcade*
stick use	stretch it do.	Dry	the nice	be	go	sell	do.

yap	*hị're*	*yabǝ petę'*	*kị·*	*ta'hǝre*	*yukse'*	*hị·*	*ǫ'watca*
Wood	the	wood [locust] flat	the	make	spoon	the	use

kai'kai"	*hade.*	*nuyą"*	*kị·*	*tcuwi'*	*hị·wi·*	*ta'ye*	*ka'tcade.*	*nuyą'*
scrape	do.	Grease	the	much	the	soap	make do.	Grease

kị·ye	*ya'tci*	*tcirik ka'tcade*	*mi·ro'*	*kǝre"*	*ka'tca*	*de*	*tǝpa'haksǝ*
the	ashes	run make do	strong	good	make	do	clothes

te'resǝri'sǝde.
out clean do.

FREE TRANSLATION

(First) skin the cow. Put ashes and salt on the cow hide. Take out the fluid-in-the-head (brains) of the cow and rub it on the hide. Put it in the groud leaving) it in the ground for four days. Take it out and the hair will be removed, wash it to clear off the hair. Then hang it up stretching it on a frame. When nicely dried it will sell well. Of flat-wood (locust) make a spoon, use it to scrape (the hide). The grease (scraped off) make into a lot of soap. Run the grease into ashes, make it strong (soap) and wash clothes with it.

101. Catching Fish by Use of Poison. (I)

di·	*tǝro'*	*samụtu"*	*nanena"*	*yi'wi·*	*web'hada'he".*	*uni'k'*
I	little	when	father my	fish some	catch went.	Then

di	*tca'wahę".*	*warupi's*	*yamụ'bagik*	*yi·'*	*sakhomi'hohę".*
I	fish.	Walnut bark	in water put	fish	top come.

yą'tca	*haktco'*	*kusayę"*	*yą'tca*	*hisuyi'*	*ba'gi·hę"*	*warupis'*
Branch	hole	there	branch	edge	out in	walnut bark

haktco'	*kusa'yę"*	*yap*	*o'wǝtca*	*mu'kri·hę".*	*unia't'*	*yi·'*	*sakho'*
hole	there	stick	using	stir up.	Then	fish	top

sakho mi·hohę͏ᵖ.	*unia't͏ᶜ*	*webipkę͏'*	*tcitcoyi'tcehę͏ᵖ.*	*uniat*
top	come.	Then	catch shoot	very much cause.	Then

atkowa'rihę͏ᵖ	*tuska'ktci*	*patki'*	*pą͏ᵖi·hę͏ᵖ'*	*yi'itu'wi·hę͏ᵖ.*	*uniat*
gather	bucket	big	full	fish little some.	Then

dugi·na'munt	*tce'ehę͏ᵖ*	*dugi·na'munt*	*tce·ehę͏ᵖ*	*yi·*
home go when	fry [they]	home go when	fry [they]	fish

tero'mi·ra'kəri	*tce·*	*i·ma'tcowa'hę͏ᵉ.*	*ya'paya'kane*	*hakutcehę͏ᵖ*
little more these	fry	taste sweet.	Day several	afterwards

yi·webəkę͏'	*mosa'ra*	*hapauko·hį͏'ha*	*yepsaksę͏'*	*atkowa'rehę͏ᵖ*
fish catch shoot	from	above a little	brush cut	heap[ed]

ya	*patki̜'*	*kəpegda'rihę͏ᵖ.*	*naci·aᵖtciriksəhę͏ᵉ.*
snake big		lying I see.	I am afraid run.

ye'ta	*yą͏ᶜci·adoᵖ?*
You	you are afraid?

FREE TRANSLATION

When I was little my father went to catch some fish. It was then that I fished. He put walnut bark[1] in the water, whereupon the fish came to the surface. It was in a deep hole in a branch of the river, there at the edge of the branch he put walnut bark in the hole, stirring it up by using a pole. Then the fish began coming to the top of the water. Thus he was able to catch, by spearing them, a large quantity. He gathered a large bucket full of them, some big some little fish. Then going home he fried them and the smaller ones tasted sweet. Several days after when he was spearing some fish from a little ways above here, I saw a big snake lying on some heaped-up brush. I was frightened and ran away! You! Are you afraid (of them)?

102. Fish Shooting with Bow and Arrow. (I)

yi'ye'e'	*yantca'moᵓnaᵖ*	*itcikatų͏ᶜ*	*i·yuᵖi·ye*	*yiᵖkę͏ᵖehę͏ᵉ.*
People	creek branch	go to	bow little	take with	fish shoot.

kuri'yip	*tcuwi·ᶜtcəhę͏ᵖ*	*itusta'kətci*	*tugba'gi·hę͏ᵖ*	*dugi·na'nt*
Sometimes	much get	bucket	in put	home come

hi'ri·ᵓhi·hę͏ᵖ	*wįyą͏'hę͏ᵖ.*	*wą*	*ki·nt͏ᶜ*	*dorab͏ᶜ*	*hi·tci·ᶜre*	*tcupki·*	*sahę͏ᵖ*
cook them	eat.	Arrow	the	iron	sharp	end	at

ǫwtcaᵖ	*yi·ᵖ*	*keᵖehę͏ᵖ.*
using	fish	shoot.

---

[1] Juglans nigra.

The people used to go down to the branch of the creek taking a little bow with them to shoot fish. Sometimes they would get many, and put them in a bucket. Coming home they would cook and eat them. They would shoot the fish using a cane-arrow with a sharp iron at the end.

103. Trapping Fish with Baskets. (I)

*u'tkaniduko*ⁿ	*yęye't*	*yi'*	*wasap*	*ta·*ⁿehę*ⁿ	*yi·tcoyi'*
Long time back	people	fish	basket	make	fish much

tugi·na'hę	*wasa'p*	*ki'*	*ikatca*ⁿ	*yamukai*ⁿehę*ⁿ	*kustą*ⁿ	*tukai*ⁿehę*ⁿ.
in go	basket	the	make	in water put	corn bread	in put.

uniat	*yi·*	*kint*	*tugna'hę*.	*unik*	*wasa'p*	*ki·*	*dutcę't*
Then	fish	the	in go.	Then	basket	the	take out

*ihapa'ka'i*ehę*ⁿ	*yi·*ⁿ	*ki'ye*	*we'b*ehę*ⁿ	*kuri'*ip*	*yi·*ⁿ
out on edge [of river] put	fish	the	catch	sometimes	fish

patkị'	*we'b*ehę*ⁿ	*watka'*	*yapsę*ehę*ⁿ	*wasa'p*	*katcehę*ⁿ	*tcupsę*
big	catch	white oak	wood splints	basket	make	end cut

nạ'prip	*haya'k*hahe*ⁿ.	*uni'k*	*tugina'hę*.	*wi'ya*	*qwotca*ⁿ
both	open.	And	in go.	String	using

wasa'p	*ki'*	*muwi·*ⁿehę*ⁿ	*yapmonuwi·*ⁿehę*ⁿ	*unik*	*wataraki'hahe*ⁿ.
basket	the	tie	tree ground tie	and	wash away the not.

*i·ti*ⁿ	*patkị'*	*tuka*ⁿehę*ⁿ	*uni'k*	*ta'ntcia*ⁿ	*watəra'hę*ⁿ.
Stone	big	in put	and	can not	wash away.

A long time ago the people made fish baskets. Many fish would go into the basket so made. They put it in the water, and put corn bread in it, and the fish would go in. Then they took the basket out on the edge of the river and secured the fish. Sometimes big fish would be caught. The basket was made of white-oak[1] splints. They made both ends cut open. Then (they) would go in. Using a thong they tied the basket, fastening it to earth by tying it to a tree, so that it would not wash away. A big stone would be put in it and it could not drift away."

---

[1] The baskets referred to are of the basket trap type with in-turned splints forming a funnel at the entrance.

104. *Formula to Make Fish Bite.* (II)

wasya'wa'i'ye   duksi·   u'ware də'pə'i·tca"e ųmpa'tcire   yi·
Devil's shoe-string line   put on   hook   rub on   fish

so'kəri'tcure.   dəpə'i·tca" patkane'həre.
bite well very.   Hook   big trout.

FREE TRANSLATION

Devil's shoe string rubbed on the hook and line will make the
fish bite very well. [You will] hook big trout.

105. *"Bird Brushing", Hunting with Torches.* (III)

kutci'n   hi·mana'we.   etcuwe'   sęsęa'we   etcuwe'
Bird   sleeping[1] hunt we will.   Pine   split up we will   pine

ki·   nǫwetcu'we   da   yapitį'.[2]
the   fat [in resin] much will   go   wood flat [brush heap].

pakaį'a'we   kutci'ntcuwi' hara're   yapsęmǫtu"
Some cut we will.   Bird many   here are   tree cut [old field] in

yap pətę́ kaį tcuwi're ku'tpi   ka   i'mare.   į'pi· kįˑye
wood flat cut   much   there the now sleeping.   Fire   the

duwe"yąna'we.   kutci'n səkę hę́ hagwa'we kutci'n hawo'k'tce
blinds them will.   Bird   red or kill will   bird   black

hę kutci'n wa'wə hę" ti·nde'hę"   kutci'n   hį·tu" ituse
or bird snow or bluejay or bird [song sparrow] small dove

hę". kutci'n tətemp'   kəra're.   kutci'n hi·mada'de.   pa
too. Bird all kinds   there are.   Bird brushing go do. Person

na'mənа   ka'ka"we,   yəka wi·yu'we [tcea'we hrą́'we
three   knock down will,   you carry will [fry will eat will

yawəbti·   wi·hrą́'we   kustą́'ye mi·harą́'we.] kutci'n kį·
morning the then eat will corn bread with eat will.]   Bird   the

---

[1] This denotes more than is actually said by the phrase "bird sleeping
[hunting]", for it implies that while the birds are sleeping the hunters will
take advantage of their being blinded by the torches and kill them.

[2] The variation in pronounciation of which the Catawba are guilty is
shown here. Ordinarily this would be *na ya'p petę́'*.

monobokʿha'   *du'rəde*   *di·te'mp*ᶜ1   *padu'de.*   *di·te'mpʿi*
on ground put pick [them] up do   all   some take do.   All

    payu'hade.   *ya* *nɑ'pəre* *du'yəre*2, *de'ta* *nɑ'pəre*
some [of them] take do. You two take,   I two

tcu'səre. *wa'yahəre* *tci̧'tcə* *motu̧ᵖ* *kutci'n* *i'mana'həre.* *waya*
I take. Winter it is cold when bird sleep hunt. Winter

mi' *hani·'tcəre* *dapaᵖna* *təpəhwɑᵖ* *igwa're.*   *ya'rɑ* *hi̧·*
only that do   hunt I   rabbit kill.   Summer the

   yɑtca'   *ha'awe*   *yace'* *wi'patɑ're.*   *ya'ce* *ki̧·*
water branch fishing we will eel many catch. Eel the

   hiri'a'we *wi·tca'use.*   *hi·tcəwatcu'we.*
cook we will evening. Sweet taste very will.

   eskatreᵖ *na'mənda* *yȩ'ye* *mi·ra'* *ki·ye* *yȩ'ye* *na'mənda*
   White man   three   Indian chief the Indian   three

kutci'n *hi·mana'doᵖ?* *waʾ*   *mo'nokəba'parɑ'həre.*
bird   sleeping hunt? Snow on ground covered completely.

kəri̧' *hatcu're.* *na'musatcu're.* *kutci'n* *nɑpəre'* *digwa're,* *ye'ka*
Good very it was. I like it much. Bird   two   I killed, you

nɑ'prəre *yi·gwa're.* *pa'ktəre* *hi'wo* *di'pkəre* *hi'wo* *pi'ki·kowa'rəre.*
two you killed. Five may be six may be fly away.

   yȩ *imbəre'tci* *ki̧·* *sa'retcure*3 *indite'i* *parɑ'hare.* *ya'otca'* -
   Man Indian the sorry very lose completely. Tomorrow

wa   *kohru'we.*   *ɑn* *tap'tci·ke'ŋk*   *yaotca'*   *təpȩ'*
night go again may.   Then guinea-hen tomorrow night one

  wi·ba'we *təpeᵖ* *wi'baharɑ'we* *pa* *hakwa'we* *wi·tca'uset.*
catch we may one catch and eat some kill we may tonight.

deʾa're *yaha'* *ki̧·* *təpȩ'* *wi·ba'we* *hanoyu'we*   *dukəna-*
Get lost goose the one catch may steal you may back home

  hi'ri·a'we.   *i·səne'* *sębe'rəretʿ* *təpɔ'* *hadəbaʾa'we.* *waʾa'* -
cook we may. Buzzard ancient the one find we may. Let

  kohru'we *tə'tca*4   *hacɑ'we*   *su̧w* *i·tcu'we.*
him go will cannot eat we will stinks so much will.

---

1 Note alternation of *d-* and *n-* in this term. Possibly the *n-* of *ni· te'mpʿ* is modified to *d-* through the proximity of *d-* in the preceding term.

2 When repeated this was given as *du're.*   3 *sáre-*English "sorry."

4 Note *tɑ'tcia* as Mrs. Owl (I) pronounces it.

["When the] birds [are] sleeping we will hunt [them]. We will split the pine with much fat [resin] in it and go to a wood flat [brush heap]. We will cut some. There are many birds there now sleeping in the wood flat [brush heap] in the old field where much wood has been cut. The fire blinds them. We will kill a red bird or black bird or snow bird or blue jay or the small bird [song sparrow] and also the dove. There are birds of all kinds. Do go bird brushing. If three persons go and knock down birds they will put them in a sack. I will carry or you will carry it. [In the morning we will fry them and eat them with corn bread.] Then put the birds on the ground, pick them up, all taking some. All take some of them. You take two and I take two. In the winter when it is cold is the only time we hunt birds when they are sleeping. In the winter I hunt rabbits, kill them. In the summer we will go fishing for eels in the water branch. We catch many eels and we will cook them in the evening. They will taste very sweet.

Three white men, the Indian chief and three Indians went out to hunt sleeping birds ? The ground was completely covered with snow. It was very good, I like it very much. I killed two, you killed two. Five, maybe six flew away. The Indian man was very sorry to lose them completely. Tomorrow night we may go again. Then tomorrow night we may catch one guinea hen. We may kill some tonight. The goose that got lost we may catch and bring back home and cook it. We may find an old buzzard but we will let him go. He stinks so much we cannot eat him.

106. Bush Netting. (III)

yɑ hye'	sapəku'tɘre	yapyo'tca	yi'ᵖtasi	wi'bɘre
Water	muddy	tree [branch] using	fish netting	catch

hani'tca kį·	yi· wi'bɘre tɘ'tci·ᵖ	do'pa	yanɑ'we	sapəku'tɘtcu'we
so done	the fish caught cannot	anything	see will	muddy so will be

yɑ'ye	sa'piku'tɘrehę'	yi· ųta'sihę'	yi· we'bi·hę'	hį·tu'waha'hę".
water	muddy is	fish netting or	fish catching	blind (eye no).

hawapɑᵖhɘre	nu'wi·ihᵖ	yi· tcuwi!	wi·ba'we	dukna-
Be filled up	tied together	fish many	catch will	back home go

tcę'awe	hɑwapɔ'a'we	yɑ'p	kį·	tcipse'-
fry them will	get filled up full will	tree branch	the	ends

nowi'ire	*yę bəri'tci*	*yanda' kusa*	*dəpę́*	*i·saka⁰əre*	*yusəre⁰əre*
tied together	men	stand in middle	one	each side	dragging

yi'tcuwi¹	*we'bəre*	*yi·*	*i·ta'si·*	*ną́'prəre*	*pitcəną́'prəre.*
fish many	catching	fish	netting	two	ten two [twenty].

hane'həre.
That's end.

FREE TRANSLATION

In muddy water, using tree branches for netting fish is a method of taking fish. They cannot see anything because the water is so muddy, the muddy water (enables) them to be netted and caught while blinded. (When the bush net) is filled up the fish are tied up, many fish will be caught, and taken home to be fried and we will be filled up full. The top ends of the branches are fastened together and men standing in the middle (of the stream) and one on each bank dragging it along. Many fish will be caught by fish-netting, (sometimes) twenty-two. That's the end.

107. Opossum Hunting. (III)

wi·tca'wasə⁰	*dəpəhna'we*	*təpətustərę̨⁰.*		*pawi·baharą́'we*
Tonight	go hunt will	opossum.	Some we catch and eat will.	

tą́'si	*kərį́'həre*	*witi¹*	*pu⁽pu⁽ⁿhade*	*pase⁰*	*dugho'rəre*	*ya'p kį·*
Dog	good	horn	blow do	ax	take along	tree the

kaį́'hade.	*hatci'k*	*ma ho+*	*hapkǫ'tci·re.*	*yap patkį́'*	*hapda're*
cut.	Listen	ma! ho!	he is up a tree.	Tree big	up went

wotka' patkį·	*hapda're*	*tą́tci·*	*ya'pi*	*kaįsa're.*
white oak big	up went	cannot	tree	I cut down.

FREE TRANSLATION

Tonight we shall go opossum hunting. We may catch some and eat them. A good dog, blow the horn, and an ax take along and cut down the tree! Listen, ma! ho! he is up a tree. He went up a big white oak tree, a tree I cannot cut down.

108. Making Corn-Husk Mats. (III)

kusta' ktapse'	*kį̇·ye*	*kusta' ktapse' tahəre.*	*yę́ ka*
Corn-shuck floor	the	corn-shuck floor make.	Catawba

ta⁰are.	*daha' pi·tu̧həre*	*da' pi·ka*	*ata' wohatci·de.*
the make.	Cloth piece	cloth	bind edge cause do.

7

The corn-husk mat is made of corn-husks for the floor. The Indians make them. With a piece of cloth you bind the edge.

PREPARATION OF FOOD

109. Recipe for Parched Corn Soup. (III)

ku's	apsa'de.	ti'ti'ʰhade	ti'ti'səmi'	hatcade.	tukəse'
Corn	parch	do.	Beat it up do	beat it fine	cause it to be.	Pot

mǫbo'kʻhade	haro'tcide.	ta's	atcę͟ʔ	mǫbokʻhade.	tus	pat kį'
in put do	boil make it.	Salt	a little	in put do.	Pot	large

mǫtcę' hǝde	hara'ri·we	yuk se'	hatci	kǝruga'we	dǝtę͟'
n pour do	dance around it	spoon	using	drink we will	all

mǫkǝruga'we.
on ground drink we will.

Parch the corn. Beat it up until has become fine and soft. Put it in a cooking pot and make it boil. Put a little salt in with it, and pour it into a large pot. (Then) we will dance around it, and using a spoon drink it all sitting around on the ground drinking it.

110. Recipe for Lye Hominy.[1] (III)

kus	sǝra'hę͟ʔ	kus	pis	sǝre't'ha.	yatci	m͟ʻ	bokʻa'we
Corn	husked [is]	corn	skin pulled off.		Ashes	in	put will

haru'ukǝrihowe.	kus	pisę͟ʔ	kǝri'ʰhowe.	kus	katkata'we
boil good will.	Corn	skin	good will be.	Corn	shell out will

pa' po'harǫwe.
pour out and eat will.

Husked corn is corn with the skin or shell removed. We put it in ashes and boil it well. The corn skin is good. So we shell the corn, pour it out and eat it.

---

[1] This is the Catawba method of preparing the famous corn food known to the Creeks as *sofkee*.

111. Rules for Cooking Beans. (ɪ)

nuntce′ ko′ko hiri·sə′rehę̨ꞏ du‘rą′rehę̨ꞏ.   tusə   pąse″
Bean snap cook I   eat we.   Pot leg cut [cooking pot]

duġ bɑ′k səhę̨ꞏ wi·dyo′ mukaisəhę̨ꞏ.   awa′¹ ną′prihę̨ꞏ hiri·‘səhę̨‘.
in put I   meat mix with I.   Hour two   cook I.

yapsenuyą́   *kuni′tco*   *saġ bɑ′ksę̨hę̨ꞏ,   nu′yą*
Board-for-food [table]   nice very [set]   down put I,   eating

de tɑ′yɑt itu′s ndɑpkatɑ′hyę̨ꞏ.   itus pakatsɑ′t wę̨′djɑ’kake′re.
done   pot   I wash.   Pot breaking I   pay must.

FREE TRANSLATION

Snap-beans² I cook to eat. I put them in a pot, and mix them with
meat. For two hours I cook them. I set the food-board [table] nicely
and call them to come and eat. When finished eating I wash the pot.
If I break the pot I must pay for it!

112. Rules for Cooking Crawfish. (ɪ)

i′sę̨ꞏ   itcwa′ hę̨ꞏ.   nuyą́′k mǫbɑ′ġihę̨ꞏ tas atce′ mǫbɑ′ġihę̨ꞏ
Crawfish sweet.   Grease in put salt little in put

mukri′ꞏ ehę̨ꞏ.   iyą́′ mǫtut‘ i·si′k·ahę̨ꞏ.
stir.   Done when   red.

FREE TRANSLATION

Crawfish are sweet. Put in gre se with a little salt and stir. When
they are done they are red.

113. Rules for Cooking Hoe-cakes. (ɪ)

kuspa″ ǫwətcɑꞏ tas atce′ mǫbɑ ꞏihę̨ꞏ.   yą́′ye mǫtce″ihę̨ꞏ
Corn meal using salt little in pu .   Water in pour

ope′tcehę̨ꞏ itu′s mǫpo’ę̨ꞏ   kustą̨ꞏ kɑ′tcehę̨ꞏ iktą́′hę̨ꞏ
mix   pot   in down put corn baked make.   Make

mǫpo″ehę̨ꞏ.   iksɑ″ ǫwətcɑꞏ tɑ″tɑ’e′ petę̨′re tcahę̨ꞏ kustą́′ kị·
in down put. Hand using   pat   flat make corn bread the

---

¹ Derived from English.
² Only the whitebeans are raised by the Catawba, who call them "snap-
beans". The neighboring Cherokee, however, cultivate at least six varieties.

7*

mǫpo'e'mǫtu't   *bɑgre'retcehę*.   *kustą' yaso*.   *yaso'mǫtut*
in down in   round make.   Corn bread done.   Done when

hitcwa·hę.
sweet.

FREE TRANSLATION

Taking corn meal, put a little salt in it. Pour in water and mix it in a pot to make baked corn. Put it in to make it bake. Using the hand, pat it to make it flat and round. [Then the] corn bread is done. When it is done it is sweet.

SUPPLEMENT

The following four texts narrated by Mrs. Owl in 1913 are those referred to in the introduction as having been published in the Journal of American Folk Lore, Vol. XXVI, pp. 319—330. On a later occasion when some knowledge of the language had been gained they were analyzed and revised versions prepared. These are now included in the collection.

114. Rabbit Fails to Imitate his Host, the Bear. (I)

numę́ kị́t utaʾ dɑpəhwą́ ki·t utkǫya´, "sugnɑ´-
Bear the said [to] rabbit the he told him, "Come to my

hode´ kuri·ʿki·wi·tcaude." uni·atʿ ure´rehohyeʾ. uni·ɑ´tʿ
house to spend the day." And indeed, he did go. Then

darasa´kutce¹hi·yɑt numę́ kị·t nuyą·hi¹rihati¹ri·e.
along towards noontime bear the commenced to cook dinner.

uni·atʿ dəpa´wi·teųra´ owo´tci´yaʾ hitcəpi´tki·pʿhatirie. u´ni·atʿ
And an awl using his heel he stuck. And

nuyaŋk te´rahoti¹rie. nuyą´mutcę́ti·rie. u´nikʿ
grease came out. [Into the dinner] he poured the grease. And

nu´yą·ti·rie. uni·ɑ´tʿ dəpahwą́ kị· utaʾ, "ya¹p·oni·he·ri·mųt hode´
they dined. And rabbit the said, "On a certain day come

su´gna ma ho´de kre´wi·tca´ude." uni·atʿ ure´rehoʾ. dara´-
to my house come stay all day." And he went. Along

sareya´t dəpəhwą́ kị́t nu´yąheri·hati¹rie.
towards noon rabbit the dinner commenced to cook.

omətaʾʾ dəpa´wi·te´ųra o´wətcaʾ hitcəpitki¹pʿhaya´t,
Imitating [the bear] an awl he used his heel he stuck,

nu´yaŋk pa´ị̃¹hati¹rie. unikʿ hị́pa waru´phatci·me´ kan
grease none came. And his foot sick it very so that now

wa´reti¹rie.
he died.

FREE TRANSLATION

The bear spoke to the rabbit, saying, "Come to my house to spend the day." And along towards noontime the bear commenced to cook dinner. Then, using an awl, he stuck his heel with it. And grease came forth. Then he poured the grease into the dinner. And they dined. Then the rabbit said, "On a certain day come over to my house and stay all day." And so the (bear) went. Along towards noontime the rabbit commenced to cook dinner. In imitating the bear, he used an awl, and struck his heel with it. But no grease at all came forth. And his foot pained him so badly that it killed him.

115. *Opossum Outwits the Deer and the Wolf.* (I)

pa'səm[1]	ye'deresu⁰		kapowa'nki·	hi'tcwąko⁰were.
Opossum	persimmon tree	under [was] sitting		resting.

wi·dabo'ye	ma'hore		"hi'tcwado⁰ ?"
Deer	come along	"Is it (persimmon) good (he asked)?"	

"dəpe'n kəpere',		nąka·ni·de!"
"One is lying there, underneath,	eat it and see [for yourself]!"	

"ta'i·ntceyəmwi·yado⁰?"		"sak hapki·	ya·tci'rikhe'ri·ho
"How do you get them to eat?"	"Uphill		you run

yap hase'	patci·ka'iyət	nit'e'm	saho're	oni'k
tree (?)	strike	all persimmons	will come down	and

mahawą'si·hore	[enhawą'si·hore].		ore're	ǫ'tci·hę⁰
we shall both eat			He went running	bumped

oni'k	duk	hebę⁰	dukhawa'ri·hę̌.	pasəm	si·pa di'
[against it]	and	down	fell	down dead. Opossum	knife

rahę	mowąki' kho'rehę̌.		tą'si su'rie	hasa⁰hati'ri·e
went for	singing as he went along.	A wolf	stepped out [and]

tu'rehi'ndya		"tcapa'tsəsaʾ!	namo'wansə-
asked the reason [for singing].	"Nothing at all!		I was just merely

te'hę."	"hį·ya'p teruna'yədaʾ!"		"wi'dəwe
singing."	"your head I will snap off!" [said wolf.]		"A dead beast

da'niku·tsəʾ"	"atci'grət, ha'nahani'here!"	uni·a't⁽	nǫ'wątə-
I have found."	"Go on, let us go and see it!"	And	he started,

---

[1] Derived from English.

hati·ri're;   tą'si· su'rie   ti·   ra'hati'ri·re.   *wi'dwe*
turning back;   wolf   the   went with him.   Dead meat

   kəpi pi·ki'   mu·na'yət   *tcu'kha   sę' heki't ha-*
lying there when they arrived at the place   a piece   cut he

ti·ri·re   atce'kitha   ka'yəhuk   hįtmọtu' khati'-
tore off a little piece he threw in his [opossum's] face, [and] he

   ri·re.   *"ko'rahadahi' moną' de!*   *ipake'*   *pi'ki·ti·i'!*
fell down.   "Go on, roast and eat it!   Quails   flying up *tii!*

   igya'ni·motu',   *'wị·si   haure'   tci'rik-*
When you hear them [you say],   'wị·si   is coming,   I have a

   serekɑ'n'"   *pa'səm ti   wę'ki hą'rati'ri·re,   yapko'-*
notion to run away.'"   The opossum crying, went off,   wood

'koki·ti'ri·re.   ipake'   pi'ki·ti'i·hi·ti'ri·re   *moruka'-*
he broke up.   Quails flew up with a whirr, *ti·i·!* They came [near]

   hi·ti'ri·re.   *"ta'ni·ni'ᶜ?"*   *uni·atᶜ*
and alighted.   "What's the matter?" [they asked.]   And

hi'hati'ri·re tą'si· su'rie,   ha'nitci kị·ye.   uni·a't ᶜ pi'k·i·hą⁰-
he told about the wolf,   how this he had done.   Then   they flew

   rati'ri·e,   *ti'i·!. tą'si· su'rie   aki'nąkahi·ti'ri·re.*
up again and went off, *ti·i·!*   Wolf   where he was they alighted.

uni·a't ᶜ   tą'si· su'rie   kị·t   mi'cruwatci'ri·kᶜhati'ri·re.   uni·atᶜ ipake'
Then   wolf   the   got frightened and ran off.   And   quails

kị·t   agre·i'na   hi'a'katci·te'ri·e.   uni·a't ᶜ   agre'   duko'ra,
the some of them scaffold made.   And   some   remained,

wi·dyo'   kị·   ka'į·kaį·i·panati'ri·e.   ni't ᶜemp   mi·i'i'yui·ti'ri·e,
meat   the   they cut up all.   Each one   took a piece of it,

hi·ya⁰katci· ki'   moną,   wi'dyo kị'   koni'p   ha'pka'ye.
to scaffold the they went, meat the   all   up [they put].

   pa'səm   kị't   hapkai'᾽ti'ri·e   ha'pki·,   wąkọ'wamu'są-
Opossum   the   up they put him   way on top,   he was

   tcu'kọti'rie·.   wi'tca'warəyat   tą'si· surie du'hoti'ri·e   wi'-
exceedingly glad. In the evening   wolf   came back   dead

dwe   kəpikị·   mo'raka'ni·ti'ri·e.   uni·atᶜ   pą⁰eha'hę'.
beast to where it lay he went to look for it.   And there was none.

aki'rakre'   *mo'waha ka'ni·ti'ri·e*   *kuri'yip*   *iyą' surati'-*
Round about   in water he looked   by chance   [at the] edge of

ri·e.   *uni'at*   *pa'səm*   *hį'nda ya'muwaka'ni·ti'ri·e.*   *uni·a't*
the water.   And   Opossum   shadow in water saw.   Then

yamu hi'   *wąhati·ri·e*   *u'pi'tcə'hami'ʹhati'ri·e.*   *unia't*
into the water   he jumped   he dove in and came out.   And

hapa'wąhadu'grehati'ri·e.   *uni·at*   *bu'ruk wą'-*
he jumped out on the bank, looked back again.   Then   back again

hi'yą.   *uni·at*   *bu'ruk ya'muhi·wą'hahe,*   *u'pi'tcə'hami'ʹ-*
he jumped.   And   back into the water he jumped,   he dove and

hą'hi·ya.   *ya'p ha*   *kre' mǫbeʹbeʹ*   *haka'-*
came out.   Among leaves [floating]   there he bit [among them]

ni·he.   *unia't*   *pa'səmti*   *ha'pki·wą'*   *ha'ha''hatcu'kə-*
to see.   And   opossum   above sitting   laughed so hard

wąti'ri·e.   *ani·pu'k*   *hi'tcəpą*   *hu'ktcę'hak.*   *ya'ni·ti'-*
sitting [there].   And then   his slobber   fell down.   [It fell] the

ri·e.   *haka't ha'vri·hamą¹ wi'dyo mahati'ri·e.*   "*atce'*
water into.   Now   he looked up   meat   he begged.   "A little piece

huka'i·hat   *tcą'dawa're*   *tsu'kha-*
throw down   I will eat it and pretend I am dead   and we will laugh

ha'auʹ."   *uni·a't*   *hatce'ra'ə*   *huka'iʹ-*
together."   Then [he begged], "A little bigger piece   throw down

hak waru'pha   *mahi'raki·datukha.*   *kəpi'tki·*
I will grab it and fall down [pretending]."   Lying down [when this

atka'ni·ha   *ka'hǫwahati'ri·e.*   "*du'graha*
was done]   a little while   he got up.   "Again

atce'raha   *nį·t da wa'ri·yi'*   *əntsa'ga wahaha'aure;*
a little bigger piece,   I will say I am dead   surely, and we will laugh;

taru'mi·ra'ha   *huka'i'hak*   *waru'pha*   *hi'raki'daha."*
[but] a great big piece   throw down,   I'll grab it   and fall down

"*hi·mba'aki're."*   *ha'mopitki·,*
[pretending]."   "Oh, yes! that's it!" [said wolf.]   He fell down,

---

¹ The *b* was originally written down as *v*, bilabial affected by proximity of *r*.

a'tkani·ti'rie.	*uni·a't^c*	*buru'kahǫ'wą,*	*kahwą°ha,*	*"huka't*
lay a while.	Then	again he rose,	got up [and said],	"Now

tarohe'ri·	*nį't*	*tca'ndawa'ri°i·,*	*hį'tsakha'-*
the great big piece	I	will eat and pretend to die,	for certain

ha'a'u."	*uni·a't^c*	*ha^cpi·*	*pat kį'*	*wo'katara'*
we will laugh!"	Then	chunk	big	bony joint piece [he

pərąha'	*ha'bre'ha*	*"ha'nituke·do'?"*
showed the wolf]	when he looked up.	"Is this enough for you?"

uni'at^c	*"hi·mba'a·,*	*mąki'ri·re!"*	*uni·a't^c*	*hu'ki-*
And [he said],	"Yes, indeed,	it's enough!"	Then	he threw

ka°əhaya't	*waru'phama,*	*ku'rukha,*	*hi·raki·dahati'ri·re.*
it down	he [wolf] grabbed it,	he swallowed it,	and fell down.

uni·a't^c	*uri'ri· wa'ri·et,*	*du'gəre*	*ka'hǫhwąhati'ri·e.*
And	really he died,	again	he did not get up.

FREE TRANSLATION

Opossum was sitting beneath a persimmon tree, resting and eating persimmons. The deer came along, and asked him, "Are they good?" — "There is one lying there, try it yourself and see!" said the opossum. "How do you get them down?" asked the deer, (after he had tried one and found it to his liking.) "You run up the hill and down, bumping your head against the tree; then they will all come down and we shall both have plenty to eat," said the opossum. Then the deer went up the hill, and bumped his head against the tree, and he fell down dead. Now, the opossum went for a knife to cut him up with, singing as he went along. A wolf heard him, and stepped out and asked him what he was singing about. "Nothing at all!" said the opossum, "I was just merely singing." — "I will snap off your head if you don't tell me," said the wolf. "I have found a dead beast," said the opossum. "Well, go on and let us see it!" said the wolf. They started back, the wolf going along. Now, when they arrived where the dead beast was, the wolf tore off a little piece (from the guts), and threw it into the opossum's face, so that he fell down. "Go roast that and eat it!" he said. "When you hear the noise of a flock of quails rising up, tii, you say, 'Wi·nsi is coming, I guess I will run off.'" (He told the opossum to say this, in order to frighten away anybody who might be met with, who would aid him.) Then the opossum went away crying. (As he went along,) he broke some wood. This startled some quails, who flew up with a roar, tii! They came and alighted near him. "What's the matter?" they asked. Then he told them all about what the wolf had done to him. And they arose again and flew off. They went to where the wolf was, and alighted near him. The noise frightened the wolf, and he ran away (leaving the meat). Then some of the quails made a scaffold, while some remained and cut up the meat. Each one took a piece of it and went to the scaffold, until they had it all up there. Then they also put the opossum there on top. He was very glad. In the evening the wolf came back to where the dead beast was, to look for it; but none was there. He searched all about. By chance he happened near the edge of the water (where the scaffold had been made, above the river); and he saw the opossum's shadow in the water. He jumped in and dove, but got nothing. Then he climbed out on the bank again, and looked around. Then he jumped back into the water. He dove and came out. He bit among the floating leaves to see where the shadow was. The opossum sitting up above laughed so bad that his slobber fell down. (Since then opossums have always had this habit of grinning and slobbering.) It dripped into the water, and the wolf looked up. He begged a little piece of meat of the opossum. Said he, "Throw me down a little piece! I'll eat it and pretend I am dead, then we can laugh about it." (The opossum threw him a little piece.) "Throw me down a bigger piece, and I'll grab it and fall down," said the wolf. "When the opossum threw him another piece,) he fell down, lay a little while, then got up. "Now throw me a still bigger piece, and I'll say I am dead for certain, and we will laugh," said he. "Throw me down a great big piece, and I'll fall down," said he. (The opossum held out a big piece, and asked him if that would do.) "Oh, yes: that's enough," said the wolf. Then he rose again, and again said, "Now throw down that great big piece, and I'll pretend to die for certain when I eat it, and we will laugh." Now the opossum held out a big bony joint, (and asked him if that would do.) "Oh yes! certainly," said the wolf. Then he threw it down, the wolf grabbed it, swallowed it, and fell down. And he really did die, never to rise again.

116. *The Pig Outwits the Wolf.* (I)

tą'si su'rie	wi'tkərą hi·nuʼ	u'tkɔyaʼ,	"ya'p oni·he'ri·-
Wolf	fighting pig	he said to him,	"Upon a certain

mut ho'de	du'gəra	du'khode.	u'nikʻ	tu'riʼiʼya
day, come	and back	home come [come see me].	And	apple ripe

tco'yi·   *hadra'di're,*   *u'nikᶜ*   *hanato're."*   *uni·a't*
a lot   are over there,   and   we will go get some."   Then

    ure'riho'hę.   *wi·tkərą'*   *hi·nu*   *kị·t*   *ho'dye.*   *uni·a't*
he went, indeed.   Fighter   pig   the   came.   Then

tą'si· su'rie   *kị't*   *utą'*   *"det betca'tcatcuntare."*   *uni·a't*
wolf   the   said,   "I have already been there."   Then

wi'tkərą'   *kị·t*   *utaᵖ*   *tą'si· su'rie*   *kị't*   *u'tkǫyaᵖ*   *ya'p ani·-*
fighter   the   said   [to]   wolf   the   he told him   "Upon   a

he'ri· mųtᶜ ho'de."   *uni·atᶜ*   *ure'ri·*   *ya'pkuse*   *mora'yat*
certain day come."   And   he went [when] that day   arrived

hohę'.   *uni·a'tᶜ*   *wi'tkərą*   *kị't*   *utaᵖ,*   *"de't*   *be·tcatcunta're."*
came.   And   fighter   the   said,   "I have already been there."

uni·a'tᶜ   *tą'si· surie*   *kị't*   *utaᵖ,*   *"ya'p ani·ramųtᶜ*   *ho'de."*   *uni·a't*
Then   wolf   the   said,   "On a certain day   come."   And

ure'ri·   *ya'p kuse·*   *mora'yat;*   *ure'rehohę'.*   *uni·a't*
he went [when] the day   came;   he went, indeed.   And

tą'si· surie'   *kị·t*   *utaᵖ,*   *"det be'tca'tcunta're."*   *uni·a't*
wolf   the   said,   "I have already been there."   Then

wi'tkẹrą'   *kị't*   *utaᵖ,*   *"ya'p ani·ramų't*   *ho'de."*   *uni·a't*   *huka't*
fighter   the   said,   "On a certain day   come."   And   now

tą'si· surie   *kị't*   *e'hahę".*   *u'ni·ka'n*   *ya'p*   *kuse'*   *mora'yat,*
wolf   the   did not like it.   And so   day   that   arrived,

mora'hyę'.   *su'k sa'ha'*   *"ehe'mᶜ! huka't*   *yi·ntca'-*
he went.   He stepped into the house.   "Ehem'!   Now I shall have

raha'ya."   *uni·atᶜ*   *wi'tkərą*   *kị't*   *utaᵖ,*   *"yąpəsaᵖhasa're*
to eat you!"   And   fighter   the   said,   "Do be seated

hu'kwą atce'reka'de   *hukaha'*   *nu'yąhe'ri·satce're.*   *unik'*
a little while   just now   I am engaged in cooking.   And

datcą'nawapą'ᵖsutka're   *u'ni'kᶜ*   *kunka'*   *di·tro'mi·ra'yi·hiŋ'k*
I will eat a big mess   and   so now   I shall be bigger

kunkaᵖ   *yą'wapą'ᵖyu're."*   *uni·a't*   *tu'sə pąseᵖ*
and so now   you will have a big mess."   And   a cooking-pot

patkị'   *kusa·yat*   *yą'ye*   *pąhakusa',*   *ha'rotcutri'ye.*   *uni·a't*
big   standing [with] water full standing, boiling hard.   And

wi·tkərą̨   *hi·nu*   *ki̧'t*   *terąre'rą'hati·ri·e.*   *kę̨'hi·yat*   *tci·ri·khe'ri·*
fighter   pig   the   outside went.   After   a while   running

     suk sa'hati'ri·e.   *tą̨'si·su'rie*   *ki̧·*   *u'tkǫyą̨'*   *"yę̨*
he entered the house.   Wolf   the   he told him   "People

     tci·tcoyį̨'ha'a'ure!"   *uni·a't'*   *tą̨'si· su'rie*   *ki̧'t*   *uta'*   *"ta'-*
a whole lot are coming!"   And   wolf   the   said,   "Where

     tca'ru' ?"   *uni·a't'*   *wi·tkerą̨'*   *ki̧'t*   *uta",*   *"ha'wəkae'*   *na·i·re."*
shall I go?"   And   fighter   the   said,   "Hide   go."

tu'sə   *pą̨'se*   *patki̧'*   *yą̨'ye.*   *pą̨'kusa',*   *ha'rotco'-*
Cooking-pot   big   [with] water   full standing,   boiling

kusati'rie   *ha'kpą̨'hę̨'*   *sakpą̨' hakusa'hyę̨'.*   *uni·a't'*   *i'tus hi'*
hard standing   the lid   over it was standing.   And   pot-hook

       wotcya'   *tu'sə pą̨'se*   *ki̧'*   *hu'kətco'hyę̨'.*
using [took it off the fire]   cooking-pot   the   he set it down.

uni·a't'   *dugre"ha*   *uta",*   *"ha'nthode, ha'wəka'e na·i're."*   *uni·a't'*
Then   he looked back   said,   "Here come,   hide   go."   And

səwa'nkhə   *mora'hyę̨.*   *uni·a't'*   *ha'kpąhe*   *ki̧'*   *ka'rapha'.*
he rose   and went.   Then   lid   the   he slipped off.

tą̨'si· surie ki̧·   *wep'hą̨'*   *tu'sə pąse"*   *tuka'ehą".*
Wolf   the   he grabbed   [in the] cooking-pot   he put him in it.

hakpąhe   *ki̧'*   *sakpąhahyę̨'.*   *uni'k'*   *wa'ri·hę̨'.*
Lid   the   he put over [the pot].   And   he [the wolf] died.

FREE TRANSLATION

The wolf invited the pig, saying, "Upon a certain day come to visit me. Over there (where I live) are a lot of ripe apples, and we will get them." Then he did go. The pig (fighter) came (to the wolf's house), and the wolf said, "I have already been there (and back again)." (But he had not been there at all.) Then the pig said to the wolf, "Upon a certain day come (and visit me)." And when that day came, he went. Then the host (the pig) said, "I have already been there." (He lied, as the wolf had at the first.) Then the wolf said again, "On a certain day come (and visit me)." And when that day came, (the pig) went. And the wolf said, "I have already been there." Then the pig said, "On a certain day come (and visit me)." But now the wolf was angry. And so when that day came he went. He entered the house.

"Ahem! Now I shall have to eat you up (instead)." Then the pig said, "Do be seated a little while! Just at present I am cooking. And I will eat a big mess, so that I shall be bigger; and (when you eat me,) you will have a big meal." And a big cooking-pot was standing near, full of hard-boiling water. Then the host, the pig, went outside. Pretty soon he returned, running. He cried to the wolf, "A crowd of people are coming this way!" Now the wolf said, "Where, indeed, (shall I go)?" And the host said, "I will hide you!" The big pot was standing near by, full of hard-boiling water, and the lid was over it. Taking a pot-hook, he (the pig) took the pot off the fire and put it on the floor. Looking back (over his shoulder,) he shouted, "Here, come quick! I will hide you!" And the wolf jumped up and went towards him. And (the pig) slipped the lid off (the pot). Then he grabbed the wolf and shoved him into the pot, and put the lid on top. And the wolf died.

117. How the Ghosts were Heard Dancing. (I)

istci′na′	*udni·ya^ɔ*	*o′wehę^ɔ*	*hi·mu′snɑ ra′ha*	*tɘran ko^ɔ-*
My mother	told me	[that] she	my father with	outdoors

i·sa′hę'	*wi·tcaure′re*	*depę^ɔ*	*ha′tkuhɑ′*	*ha′kutci^ɔ.*	*uni·ɑ′t^ɕ*
standing	evening	one	after	sunset.	And

i′swɑ hi·a′k	*yę′yę^ɔ*	*sębe′*	*koranda′ki·*	*mɑtu^ɔ*	*yę pɑ′*
river across	people ancient		where they had lived at		somebody

i·tuske′he ka^ɔe	*tco·k*	*i·nɘhę′.*	*onika′n*	*huka′t*
pot-drum was beating	very much	heard it.	And then	now even

i′ni· ki· muntu′t	*hi′yę pɑ'eha′hę'.*
when they heard it	there was nobody [there].

FREE TRANSLATION

My mother told me that she and my father were standing outside the door one evening just after sunset. And from across the river, where there used to be an ancient Indian village, they could hear somebody drumming very hard (and people dancing and singing.) But there was nobody over there, where all the noise came from.

DATE DUE

DEMCO 38-297